Nuts in May

Books by Cornelia Otis Skinner

EXCUSE IT, PLEASE!

DITHERS AND JITTERS

SOAP BEHIND THE EARS

TINY GARMENTS

THAT'S ME ALL OVER

FAMILY CIRCLE

———

OUR HEARTS WERE YOUNG AND GAY
(with Emily Kimbrough)

Nuts in May BY
CORNELIA OTIS SKINNER

DRAWINGS BY ALAJÁLOV

Dodd, Mead & Company · New York

*Of the pieces in this book all but one, "Seaweed Sewer,"
appeared originally in* The New Yorker. *The chapter entitled "Bag of Bones" originally was entitled "Bundle of
Bones" and the chapter entitled "Kinsey Reported" originally was entitled "Trial by Kinsey" in* The New Yorker.

Designed by Stefan Salter

PRINTED IN THE UNITED STATES OF AMERICA
BY THE VAIL-BALLOU PRESS, INC., BINGHAMTON, N. Y.

FOR MY TANTE NELL

Contents

Ordeal for Sons

WHEN YOU MANAGE TO EMERGE

Ordeal for Sons

he time approaches for me to go mortify my young son by a visit to his school again, and it's a tossup as to which of us is anticipating the event with more happy apprehension. Not that I am not eager to see him; nor is there, I trust, any lack of filial warmth on his part. But in the environment of a large and pretty impressive boarding school and the atmosphere of one of those week ends when parents, teeming with tradition, run around with their offspring, doing a great many traditional things, something seems to happen which puts us both under a considerable nervous strain. My son suddenly appears to me as an amiable but utter stranger and it's obvious that I appear to him as a complete menace. In the tender bosom of home, I smugly pride myself that he looks upon me with devotion, respect and even periodic moments of admiration. In the Spartan bosom of boarding school, he regards me with tolerance, embarrassment and moments of profound shame, mingled with the sort of pitying affection one might feel for a harmless family imbecile. That he considers me anything but bright, is evinced by his letter concerning my impending visitation and containing instructions so detailed, it surprises me he didn't at the same time write his father asking him to pin my ticket on me, tip the porter and ask him to put me off at the right place. He tells me to take the night train which goes, he says, at night, from Grand Central. "When you arrive at . . ." (and, just in case my memory needed jogging, he mentions the name of the town) . . . "get off the train." (Possibly he thought I might want to stay on for the ride.) ". . . and walk through the stashion. Go to the hotel and have breakfast allthough the dog-waggon has hamburgers but then you just take coffee. I have classes all morning so do what you like. You may want a bath. . . ." (A startling suggestion coming from a small boy so allergic to them.) "At 12, take a taxi to the Alumen" (his own basic English for Alumni) "House where I'll be waiting with severall peopel for lunch." These instructions were a replica of those he sent me prior to my previous visit and as such were superfluous, the events of that pilgrimage being indelibly impressed on my memory.

That night train which leaves at night, may do so from the Grand Central, but there are certain features of it which lead one to think it would feel more at home in the Smithsonian. It winds its way northward, stopping at all stations, signal towers and, it would seem, cattle crossings, and politely pulling off at all sidings to make way for slow freights. At Lowell, the train is dismembered and the car bound for the school town is violently clashed onto a series of other trains who will have none of it and who, the moment it is coupled to them, shake it loose in apparent fury. In between times, it is taken on a scenic tour of the yards behind a switch engine driven by a novice engineer who has a lot to learn. This goes on for three or four hours, at the end of which interlude, the brakes sigh shrilly and the car, attached at last to one train which will tolerate it, heads for the north. The school is situated in the frozen heart of New England in a climate called, by those who have survived it, "bracing." You start in bracing about two A. M. and ring for the porter in the naïve hope that he will hear the bell and bring another blanket. He does neither and you continue to brace under cover of a coat, the extra pillow and that suitcase they no longer allow you to set in the aisle. By morning, you are permanently braced in a manner which, when you manage to emerge from between the icy Pullman curtains, becomes a semicrouching position.

This trip, the weather will, blessedly, be not so bracing. But the other features will be the same. Early morning in the ladies' room there will be the same jam session of females in various states of dishevelment

. . . myself in the worst state of the lot . . . lurching against one another and politely fighting for a chance at the tooth-brushing basin. This is a rude introduction to the sisterhood with whom one will be rubbing elbows for the next forty-eight hours. Last trip, my child had neglected to mention the fact that it was to be a gala week end and that a good many other parents were also coming, and I remember regarding these ladies with sentiments not untinged with venom, until, with remorseful chagrin, it occurred to me that they might be somebody's mothers, and my glare of resentment melted into a weak leer of tentative friendliness to which some responded wanly and some not at all.

This time also, I shall try to feel more charitably inclined toward whoever is in the drawing-room. Occupants of a drawing-room, unless I am one of them, rouse in me sentiments of proletarian resentment. I fix them with a Madame DeFarge stare and look about for a copy of *The Daily Worker* to brandish in their faces. The injustice of this attitude was proved by the fact that the room on this occasion was filled to bursting point by a genial family also bound for the school —mother, father, small brother entered for the year 1953, little sister profoundly bored by everything and a slap-happy Sealyham dog. The boy they were visiting turned out to be a friend of my son's . . . a fact which endeared them to me only a few degrees less than the happy moment before dinner when the father, sensing my need for such encouragement, poured me out a generous hooker of Scotch.

This time, too, I am going to know how to dress. The first trip, under the impression that I was a lone mother going quietly to visit her child at a country school, I dressed the part, as I thought, to perfection, in a tweed suit, flat shoes and an ancient coat which, after years of exposure, is beginning to look less like beaver than cocker-spaniel. With a rapidly increasing sense of inferiority, I watched the disheveled ladies of the washroom emerge from the night-in-a-Pullman chrysalis into visions of mink-coated smartness. In June, mink coats will hardly be worn, but I'm asking a friend to lend me a sable scarf in case of an emergency.

At the station, there will, I suppose, be the absence of a porter and the scramble for a taxi which is eventually shared by five beaming mothers and one lone father, anything but beaming. On the way to the hotel, there is a good deal of strained merriment. Everybody asks everybody else if they have enough room, and everybody assures everybody else that they have, although nobody has any. Then everybody asks everybody else what form their boy is in and somebody who is in the know recounts the athletic events for the day and everybody says doesn't that sound grand and everybody else says yes, doesn't it. The lone father says nothing until the taxi approaches the hotel when he comes forth with the consoling statement that he hears the school has two cases of scarlet fever.

The hotel is one of those New England hostelries

that must have been in its prime about the time of Rutherford B. Hayes. It may not be aquiver with Statler efficiency, but I find in it a good deal of pristine charm and it is perfectly comfortable. A morning spent there quietly reading a book, writing a letter or even taking that suggested bath, is restful and pleasant. Then the village clock strikes the hour of noon and I take a conveyance to the school and the "Alumen House."

Previous experience has resigned me to the deflating fact that my small boy who, at home hurtles to meet me after an absence of only half a day, with demonstrations of rapture, will now, after an absence of several months, greet me with a formal "Hi" and a bare handshake. I know better than to try to kiss him. Last time, when I leaned forward to do so, he ducked in mortification and left me smacking the air. As before, he will be waiting for me outside the front door and will conduct me inside in the manner of someone at Tattersall's bringing in a horse, the behavior of which is uncertain. The weather being milder, he will be spared the humiliation of watching me, in the process of taking off my galoshes, remove my shoes at the same time and have to stand stocking-footed for some moments in the crowded hallway. I suppose the "severall peopel" will again be three or four of his classmates to whom he will be reluctant to exhibit me and concerning whom, albeit I have never before laid eyes on them, he will expect me to know every detail. The prospect of that lunch-

eon reminds me to reserve a table. Last time, being
a novice in such matters, we found the dining room
looking like Saturday noon at Sardi's, with every table
overflowing and a line-up at the door. A gracious and
rather pretty lady asked us if we had reserved a table
and I said why no, and my son said why hadn't I, and
I countered why hadn't *he*, to which his reply was an
exasperated "Really, Mother!" Our distress was evi-
dent and the gracious lady consoled us by setting us
up a special festive board in an alcove of the library
. . . which was all right by my son who, after the
episode of the galoshes, thought it safest to keep me
quietly out of sight. Lunch was nervous but pleasant.
My child's buddies impressed me as being very nice
and I thought, somewhat fatuously, that we all got
along amazingly well; although at one point, my boy
hissed at me that I didn't have to laugh so loud. If
I did, it was due to a certain amount of strain which
I imagine they too shared. There is a technique to
carrying on social chit-chat with little boys which I am
slow at mastering. All of them were on their best behavior, which meant that most of the time, they main-
tained complete silence while I searched wildly about
in my mind for topics of possible interest. With much
too eager brightness, I asked the usual routine questions . . . where each of them came from, what colleges they were going to . . . how they liked school.
I even ventured a few remarks concerning athletics,
which, coming from me, was the equivalent of Betty
Grable discussing Relativity. They answered each

question politely and then lapsed into polite silence. Once or twice I managed to come forth with something in the nature of a quip at which they would burst out in a chorus of deafening guffaws which ceased as abruptly as they started, and there would then ensue further stretches of that polite silence. All through the meal, my son regarded me with a look which was softened by momentary gleams of appreciation, but which for the most part indicated that he thought I might at any minute start dancing a Samba on the table.

Lunch ended with no greater mishap than that I forgot to pay for it, which made him again say, "Really, Mother!" He never calls me Mother unless he is particularly ashamed of me and that week end he never called me anything else.

Lunch safely over, he pulled off the first of a series of disappearing acts which he performed at intervals during the next twenty-four hours. The school is a large one, with many buildings and vast grounds. Emerging from some hall or dormitory, he would suddenly announce that now we would go to some place with a cryptic name like Big Upper or Down Lower and, before I'd have time to ask him what he meant, he'd be gone, leaving me to wander about like a derelict until he'd appear as suddenly as he had vanished, to ask impatiently why I hadn't come along. Having some extra studying to do, he then deposited me on a settee in a sort of parents' social hall, told me not to move till he got back, and, seemingly, evaporated.

18

My time, for the most part, was beguiled by another mother . . . an imposing woman who looked like a combination of Demeter and Susan B. Anthony. She was knitting a sea-boot with such zealous efficiency, she gave the impression of doing two at the same time.

"What form's your boy in?" came from her in a clarion tone, and I realized she was addressing me.

"The First," I replied, then, noticing the slight lift to her eyebrow added, vindicatingly, "He's only just thirteen."

"Same form as my youngest," she said. Then, doubtless to put me at ease, "He's eleven."

"A Quiz Kid!" was what I wanted to say, but being a lady, merely inquired if he were her only child.

"Mercy no," she retorted. "I have five. All boys. All of them went here."

"How wonderful," I murmured.

"Their father went here before them," she continued and, being stuck for another reply, I came out with another "How wonderful."

She then started a dissertation on the subject of the school. Did I think Mr. So-and-So in the Whatsis Department was as good as old Mr. Whosis had been, and, to my mind, did Dr. X preach as good a sermon as Dr. Y? I had to confess my ignorance on such matters and the horrid fact that this was my first visit to the place. If I had admitted to never having known about the Fourth of July, she could not have looked more horrified. But she proved to be a kindly sort, and after her initial shock, she launched forth in a detailed narrative history of the school and its traditions in the simple language of a missionary telling a heathen child the story of Christmas. This hour of instruction was cut short by the arrival of my son who said it was time for hockey practice and would I care to watch. Thanking the Mother of Men for her enlightening information, I set forth with my child who, the moment we got to territory totally unfamiliar to me, again disappeared. I wandered on aimlessly, passing stray professors and groups of boys who looked at me as if they wondered if my attendant knew I was loose. Some of the mink-coat mothers also passed and we bestowed on one another that sickly smile which can be taken for recognition or pure imbecility. After a time, my offspring hove in sight armed with skates and a stick and told me to follow him. Hockey was being played on a pond some hundred yards beyond us and the people I had passed were all heading for the barrier, which seemed to be the vantage place for watching the game. Once arrived at the pond, however, my son started leading me off in an oblique direction. When I shyly asked the reason, he said he didn't want me near the barrier . . . that I might get in the way, or fall down or otherwise make myself conspicuous. His method of making me inconspicuous was to station me off on a remote and windy promontory. A strange, solitary figure, silhouetted against the snow, I felt like that picture of Napoleon overlooking Moscow. I could hardly see what was going on, much less make out which of the distant swirling figures was my child, which, perhaps, was just as well as it saved me the anguish of seeing him make a goal on his own side which counted some sort of colossal penalty and made him a pariah for the remainder of the game. On my forthcoming visit I am told the sport will be boat racing and I suppose by way of making me inconspicuous, I shall be placed in a tree.

After hockey, we made a brief sojourn to his room, which isn't a room but a sort of cubicle in a long dormitory. It looked like the East Coast of Florida after a hurricane and I offered to neat it up a bit for him. But he said no, if I did, he'd never find anything in it. So, with a shuddering glance at a mud-caked shoe reposing on a pillow and a toothbrush handle jammed into a jar of peanut butter, we left.

Next morning was Chapel, a very charming and moving ceremony which takes place at eleven. My son, although he knows I am the soul of punctuality, told me it was at ten-fifteen, but that I'd better get there by ten. I did, and found the place locked and deserted. Nor was there any sign of my child. After a time of sitting like Leah the Forsaken on the chapel steps, waiting for the doors to open, he appeared, greeted me with one of those ardent "Hi's" and said "Come on, I'll take you to your place." He sings in the choir and I was hoping for a good view of him. However, he led me to the visitors' gallery where he placed me in a far corner of the back row. When I inquired why I couldn't sit in the front row he replied, "Because" . . . an irrefutable answer I myself have resorted to so often with him, I hadn't the nerve to pursue the matter further. Perhaps he was right in putting me off in a corner. Little boys in white surplices marching down the nave of a chapel, their clear young voices raised in song, make me cry quite badly and I was glad, for his sake, nobody could see me.

After Chapel, came the ordeal of interviewing certain terrifying powers that were, concerning his work. My boy is not of the stuff that Phi Beta Kappas are made of and his marks have been a source of anguish for him, his family and, I suspect, his instructors. I had forced him into making an appointment for me with the assistant headmaster who acted as sort of dean, holding jurisdiction over the students' academic welfare . . . or, in our case, ill-fare. He seldom, they said, came into direct contact with the boys but ruled their destinies from an Olympian distance. He sounded extremely awesome and I pictured him as something between Erasmus and Zeus, hurling down on the student body thunderbolts or diplomas as he saw fit. At the prospect of my impending interview, my child was in a panic which I shared with equal acuteness. I was convinced that he would expel my son and me along with him and my knees buckled as I neared his office, at the threshold of which my offspring turned tail and beat it. The cause of our panic proved to be a delightful, mild-mannered gentleman who with great courtesy asked me to be seated and plunged right into the matter at hand by remarking that my son's marks were not over-satisfactory . . .

to which triumph of understatement I acquiesced with sorrow. Then and there we both dismissed the painful subject and there passed a charming half hour in which we talked about Katharine Hepburn's Rosalind. At the end of this I remembered that my scholar was quaking outside and excused myself, relieved that neither of us had as yet been expelled. My scholar met me with gloomy foreboding. It was apparent that he was afraid to hear the verdict.

"What did he say?" he finally managed to ask.

"He said for you to work harder," I answered. After that we then went off to lunch, just the two of us, in the hotel where, under the influence of steak, mashed potatoes and three helpings of ice cream, his formal manner relaxed and, there being nobody he knew around, I detected a gleam of the filial affection I had feared was dead.

Time came for my train. I dropped him in front of his dormitory, where was gathered a group of upper classmen. He tried to say good-by in the frozen style of his previous greeting, but in the language of departing there is no equivalent of "Hi," so he murmured an awkward "Be careful." Then he turned to leave, rushed back as if he'd forgotten something and, flinging his arms about me in a sudden tackle, smacked me shamelessly on the cheek.

I guess this impending trip will be quite similar. I shall ask the wrong questions, say the wrong things and generally shame him. In conversing with upper classmen, I shall again adopt that hearty tone of

23

voice which, according to my son, sounds as if I were on a quarter-deck in a stiff gale. I shall again be deserted in unfamiliar portions of the grounds, I and the mink-coat mothers, now in summer prints, will again leer sheepishly at one another and I shall again weep profusely over Chapel. Some long-suffering master will again discuss with me my child's mental progress . . . or lack of it. And it will all be quite charming and rather awful. But I'm going to do it. And I guess the reason is, I wouldn't miss it for anything.

Actors Will Do Anything

IT WAS IMPOSSIBLE TO TURN HIM OFF

Actors Will Do Anything

eople on committees are constantly asking actors to contribute their hours, talents and energies to participate in all manner of extracurricular shindigs in the nature of charity benefits, patriotic pageants, club smokers and local community whoop-la which don't concern them in the least. And actors who, generally speaking, are compliant creatures and would blandly agree to go over Niagara in a barrel provided they were asked long enough in advance, find themselves doing many surprising things which were certainly not what they had in mind in those clear-eyed apprentice days when, with a volume of Stanislawski clutched to their hearts, they dedicated themselves to the Muse of Drama. Every so often the enterprising chairman of the Arts and Interests Commit-

tee of some prosperously distinguished woman's club
takes it into her marcelled head that it would be
heaps and heaps of fun to pull off what, in an in-
spired moment, she has decided to call Theatre Night.
This inspiration may result in a gala of various forms.
It may mean a large dinner at which a leading critic,
acting as toastmaster, gives his witty, routine speech
on "What's Wrong with the Theatre of Today" and
then introduces a number of none too comfortable
stars and featured players who, in turn, utter con-
fused little speeches, saying how glad they are to be
there, which they're obviously not, and inadvertently
getting in a plug for his or her current show. Or it
may be a lively evening of debate, say of the Broadway vs. Hollywood formula, with representatives of
both entertainment Meccas on hand to banter good-
naturedly with one another in a rambling verbal bout
that gets circuitously nowhere, while again a few
captured notables of stage and screen sit about on
gilt chairs wondering what the hell they're doing
there, responding to introductions with gum-bared
smiles and squirming with profound discomfort when
one of their fellow Thespians, at the request of apparently nobody, suddenly gets up and volunteers to
give them Hamlet's advice to the Players. Further
forms that Theatre Night can take are the informal
presentation of a play ("informal" merely means that
everybody, including the cast, wears formal evening
clothes), or it may be a series such as Great Scenes
from Great Dramas, or it may be one of those intel-

lectual jam-sessions known as a "reading." And I feel compelled to point out, more in wistfulness than in indignation, that on all these occasions, the professional participants are never paid a cent for their participation . . . their reward being presumably a generous helping of that fun which is to be had in such abundant heaps.

I have only too frequently found myself involved in one of these evenings of cultural fun and frolic. One in particular, which took place a number of years ago, remains especially clear in my memory. It was sponsored by a club which shall be nameless but which, it is safe to say, comprises the cream of Manhattan's feminine intelligentsia. In other words, an invitation from this source came in the nature of a fairly distinguished summons and an appearance before it was not to be passed off with the same careless ease with which one made that graceful little speech accepting an honorary membership in the Dingbat University Players. My summons came by telegraph, sent by the head of the entertainment committee. She happened to be a good friend of mine. She was also one of those persons of whom it was remarked with a certain degree of reverence in lay circles that she was "once on the stage." The telegram, an exuberantly lengthy one, informed me that she had secured the manuscript of a thrilling and beautiful play, written in blank verse . . . but so good you'd never know it was blank . . . based on the life of the Dowager Empress of China. The playwright, a distinguished

29

authoress, had graciously consented to allow a group
of actors to read it aloud at a club night in late March.
She was assembling the rest of the cast, but, meanwhile, would I wire immediate assurance that they
could count on me for the part of the Empress? Pleased
and flattered, I wired back a quick "Sure." It sounded
good. Moreover, I was touring the Pacific Coast, it was
January and a New York club night in late March
seemed as remote as China itself. I never gave it another thought until my return to town some ten days
before the projected evening, when I received a
breathless telephone call from the lady procurer. She
had assembled the cast and it was a dream one. She
had told them all to be at my apartment Friday at two
o'clock for a first reading. Friday was one day distant
and I asked if I might please have an advance copy of
the script in order to familiarize myself with the part
. . . a proposal to which she reacted with shocked
amazement. I might have been a layman asking Joseph
Smith for an advance copy of the Book of Mormon. My
friend is a charming and intelligent woman but prone,
as are certain people connected with the theatre, to
shroud in terrific mystery any forthcoming production,
even one of an amateur nature. Such people have a
way of treating a new script as though it were a cipher
copy of the enemy code. The play, I was given to
understand, was not to be trusted out of her hands. It
had been a big concession on the part of the authoress
to allow us to do it at all. We mustn't even talk about
it outside of the club, as obviously the piece would

eventually be done on Broadway . . . why, and she lowered her voice to a whisper as she pronounced the name of a well-known star who had kept it on option for over a year. All of which, she abjured me, was strictly under my hat. I told her I wasn't wearing a hat, but I crossed my heart and hoped to die if I ever breathed a word of it to Sam Zolotow.

The following Friday she arrived early at my apartment, bearing two enormous suitcases. She informed me they contained the costumes which were thrillingly beautiful and absolutely authentic. Of their authenticity I felt reasonably assured. The lady had just spent four months in China and was a personal friend of Lin Yutang's which, if not establishing her completely as an authority on Sinology, was at any rate impressive. Of their thrilling beauty I had yet to judge. Like the script, they were shrouded in mystery, or, to be more accurate, in muslin dress bags. They were not to be revealed until the day of the performance, but, meanwhile, she would like to store them in a closet. My apartment was not large and the only closet not already jammed to bursting point was the one in the library. Here my friend hung up the shrouded garments, locked the door, put the key in her purse and kept it there . . . a curious act of mistrust which didn't make much of a hit with me. It made even less of a hit with my husband on his return from the office, for the closet was where we kept our entire liquor supply.

Soon after this, the other actors began assembling.

To judge by their amiable but tentative manner, it was obvious that they were all as foggy as I was about the general goings-on. The cast was indeed dazzling. The only possible criticism that might have been leveled at it would have been not from any histrionic viewpoint, but from a typing angle. The characters of the play were, naturally, all Chinese. It was therefore a little surprising to find that Vincent Price was to contribute his golden Saxon charm to the part of the Empress' faithful lover . . . (He had a name like Sing-Low or Hing High . . . I confess to having forgotten a good many of the details). Margalo Gillmore was blondly lovely as the Emperor's Discarded Wife, a lost flower of the court. Jane Wyatt, blue-eyed and shell-pink-cheeked, was a daughter-in-law with a name on the Plum-Blossom or Bamboo-Shoot order. Joseph Holland, another Nordic type, was the Chief Eunuch, which caused a good deal of merry badgering. There was a red-headed actor who played a narrator in the person of a Lord Prime Minister and three or four others in minor parts with appearances equally typical. The heir to the Dragon Throne, the boy Emperor, was in the eight-year-old hands of little Peter Miner, the son of Frances Fuller and Tony Miner. He and I being the only dark-haired members of the cast were more typical. I was even more typical than Peter owing to the fact that I was suffering at the time from a make-up allergy that made my eyelids puff up in a manner which, if less Manchu than Mongolian, was at least Asiatic.

My friend made a pleasant speech of welcome, told us we were wonderful and that the play was wonderful and suggested we do a quick run-through. She then passed out the scripts. There were only four copies which meant that we had to share them in friendly huddles reminiscent of the Della Robbia choir boys. Our quick run-through began at 2:15. By 4:30 we hadn't finished the second act. The play was a fine example of poetic drama but in length it made "Strange Interlude" and "The Iceman Cometh" look like curtain-raisers. We said it was all lovely but couldn't it stand some cutting . . . a suggestion of vandalism which my friend seemed to consider on a par with ripping out pages from a Shakespeare folio. The authoress, she said, would never stand for it. The ladies of the club, we countered, would never stand, or rather sit, for a four-hour play-reading no matter how brilliant the readers or how beautiful the play. In the end, she yielded and departed with a wave of farewell and the words, "All right, my pets. It's in your hands. Do with it as you see fit."

The pets who saw fit were Margalo and myself and what we did was the last thing the authoress could have wished to have happen to her brain-child, for we cut at least two thirds of it. The opus was a detailed account of the career of China's picturesque ruler from the time she first entered the palace as a slip of a singsong girl, to the end of her reign as the deified old dowager. It was also a pretty detailed account of what went on in China over that period and

33

certainly an awful lot went on. Margalo and I, finding the love story far more theatrically effective than
the historic events, blandly dispensed with the latter.
We cut out all political implications no matter how
moot. A neat stroke of the pencil disposed of the Boxer
Rebellion and we laughingly eliminated the scene
depicting the downfall of the Manchu Dynasty. World
War No. 1 we dismissed as being a superfluity. Our
one concession to history was to keep in the incident
of the burning of the missionaries during an embassy
garden party, as being first-rate theatre. When next
the cast met for a further run-through, our streamlined
digest proved very effective. The most affective aspect
we thought was that it took only an hour and twenty
minutes straight reading which, we were certain was
quite long enough for reader and listener. We had
worked long and conscientiously over it. As a cast too
we worked long and conscientiously over the rehears-
ing of it. Although we were spared the labor of memorizing, our integrity as Grade A actors demanded that
in reading it we give it our professional all. It took up
most of our spare time. If some of us occasionally wondered why in God's name we were knocking ourselves
out for a single evening's edification of the members
of the X. . . . Club, we were ladies and gentlemen
enough not to voice it.

The dress rehearsal took place the afternoon of the
performance. An hour or so beforehand, my impresario
friend arrived to collect the costumes from the closet
where for a week they had remained locked up with

our liquor. Nobody had been permitted a glimpse of them, the reasons for which I shall never know unless it was for motives of putting us in the mood of the Mysterious East. They were revealed to us behind the closed doors of the club ballroom and my friend was right they were thrillingly beautiful. Ancient garments of exquisite colors and dazzling embroidery, each could have been a collector's item. Mandarin robes and skirts for the men, and for the women, slim high-necked coats and trousers. For headgear, the men had black Cantonese skull-caps (Vincent's blond hair contrasted nicely with his), while the women wore real flowers which gave them a sort of Confederate belle appearance and that too was pretty. Having the role of the Empress, I was allotted a magnificent jeweled arrangement like a bishop's mitre about to turn into a birdcage. From the crown of it sprang a lot of wired-out doodads that tinkled in windbell tones when they shook which, during the performance, they did quite a lot.

The stage was a three-level platform erected at one end of the room. There being no curtain, we were to file in like a cut-down choral society and take our places in a triple line-up. Our seats were oriental couches, very stiff, very severe and so wide, if you had attempted to lean back, you'd have eventually lain prone. For lecterns, an antiquarian had loaned a number of teakwood tables. These were doubtless Chinese as all get out but they were also of a height suitable for a kindergarten class, coming barely up to the knee, which was fine by me as it meant I didn't need my glasses. It was, however, awkward for Vincent who shared the same script and who suffered with no such arm's-length vision. Both being the soul of tact, during our scenes together we kept the manuscript politely seesawing to each other's sight levels.

The play was to be read straight through without intermission. Musical interludes would indicate the breaks between acts. The only complications to arise during rehearsal were in regard to the musical interludes which were furnished by a quiet scholarly gentleman named Mr. Li (pronounced Lee). Mr. Li sat on an outer edge of the platform and, accompanying himself on a small frail instrument uncomfortably reminiscent of the cigar-box 'cello of the late W. C. Fields, burst into curious song at given moments. Mr. Li occasionally took a few moments that hadn't been given and once he'd start in with a song, it was almost impossible to turn him off. His English was limited to the point of non-existence and he apparently didn't understand occidental gesticulation. It would have seemed a breach of international good will to have nudged or shaken him. We just had to keep quiet until he got through. The songs, it seems, were every bit as authentic as the costumes, although they were a good deal more difficult to appreciate. Chinese music as an acquired taste strikes me as being nowhere near on a par with olives. Mr. Li sang (at least, that's what one assumed he was doing) a good many selections. I recall in particular a sad, wailing number which we were told was a song of spring, and an extremely lively sort of jig which was a funeral dirge and which Mr. Li executed with a broad smile. Eventually the lady in charge, my friend, through some kind of cultural pidgin communication, straightened things out, and we disbanded only to reassemble some two hours later for the show itself.

It, I am happy to report, went extremely well. In the words of one of the more ecstatic members of the entertainment committee, it was a *success* that was definitely *fou*. The ladies of the club, along with their guests and a sprinkling of rather sheepish husbands, followed our efforts with gratifying attention, expressing their interest by means of those little vocalizations of approval peculiar to the predominantly female audience, and casting momentary bright smiles at the authoress who, it seems, was a fellow member. That distinguished lady sat smack in the front row and listened with an expression of complete dead pan. It was glaringly apparent that she didn't in the least care for the cavalier manner in which we had cut her play. All of us carefully avoided looking in her direction. During the course of the evening only two untoward incidents occurred. One was a startling moment when Vincent, due to the excessive heating effects of his costume which was encrusted with gold embroidery and thickly padded like a monumental tea-cozy, was suddenly seized with an unendurable itching of his chest and involuntarily thrust his hand down through the opening below the collar. Realizing it would hardly do to be caught scratching, he resorted to the subterfuge of reaching into an inner pocket for his handkerchief. It was a good idea but somewhere in the deep layers of venerable padding, his hand caught in a rip and when, after a desperate struggle, he managed to yank it forth, some hunks of cotton wadding shot out and showered down in delicate particles, some onto the teakwood table, one or two into my face. With the player's sense of anything in an emergency, we both pretended it was intentional timing for the incident occurred during the Winter Scene when the Land was White with Snow and the Yangtze a Pavement of Ice. I don't know how convincing we were, but at least nobody laughed.

The other incident was one which concerned young Peter Miner. And at this point I should like to pay a tardy tribute to that little boy who by now must be six foot three but who then was a mite of eight and who read his lines with unfaltering ease, intelligence and sensitivity that put us all to shame. Myself in particular. My own son, a child of the same age and the slap-happy victim of Progressive schooling, at that time couldn't read *cat*. The role of the Boy Emperor was a brief one. Peter, by the end of the first act, was ready to leave and Frances Fuller, being a sensible mother, had planned to take him off home and to bed. Beckoning from a rear exit, she managed, with a minimum of confusion, to get him off the platform during one of the more absorbing passages of Mr. Li's singing. Discreetly tiptoeing, mother and son made their way down a corridor and into the vestibule of a back entrance which was seldom used except on occasions such as weddings or coming-out teas. They went through the first door which clanged to behind them and then started to open the heavy outer portal which gave onto the street. It was firmly locked. There was nothing to do but go inside and find another exit, so Frances turned to open the inner door, which having a safety catch, by this time was also locked. They found themselves trapped in a grim little cubicle, airless and unlighted. What made it especially hideous was the fact that on either side were radiators which were going full blast. There was no way of turning them off, no bell to ring and no means of summoning help except by pounding or shouting, which would have disrupted the performance back in the ballroom and that, they realized, had a full hour more to run. The heat was of a degree that would have more than satisfied the most hardened habitué of a Turkish bath. Peter gasped for breath and began turning an alarming shade of green. His mother thought he might be going to add further drama to their predicament by throwing up.

Spreading his coat on the floor, she made him lie down with his nose against the door-sill, getting what he could of the sliver of cold air coming through from outside. She herself took a braced stance against the wall and resigned herself to the inevitability of a fainting spell. Fortunately the outer door was of glass and they were eventually rescued by a humanitarian taxi driver who, spying the prostrate form of Peter and the rapidly wilting appearance of his mother, and suspecting some sort of foul play, got out of his cab, sized up the situation and found a janitor who liberated them at the moment they both were about to pass out.

Oblivious to this crisis, the rest of us wound up our performance, after which we were shepherded to a reception room where the ladies of the club buzzed happily around the authoress and my friend, congratulating them both on the success of the evening. Now and then someone told some of us that we had done nicely, too. But for the most part, we stood off at one side in an uncomfortable huddle until Margalo got the inspiration for us all to leave and go over to a nearby bar, which we did. We there got pleasantly ossified and swore a solemn oath never again to go in for any more amateur activities. The next morning, as I was nursing a hangover, a telegram arrived from a lady in Chicago. In June their community was putting on a pageant of the Opening up of the West and they wanted me to come out and represent the Spirit of the Pioneer Woman. Oh, well, I mused after I'd sent back my reply, June was a long way off. It might never happen.

Family Blessing

MOTHER UTTERED A BREATHLESS "MY!"

Family Blessing

t was heart-warming to attend a recent sailing of that festive craft, the S.S. *Vulcania* bound from New York to Naples with a passenger complement that was nostalgically prewar in character. There were the same wanly exhausted Americans, the same Italians being exuberantly typical, the same wildly running children hurtling themselves into the same gentle-eyed stewards. The same pairs of nuns stood apart discreetly whispering and the same energetic priests paced the decks with the same determined vigor. The familiar scene of amiable pandemonium quickened the sentimental pulse and set me turning back the pages of mental scrapbooks to breathless girlhood trips when Italy meant culture and fleas, gelatis and carabinieri officers, tooled leather picture frames and, if you had anything left on your letter of credit, a teagown from Fortuny.

Perhaps it was the glimpse of the black-robed clergy on their way to receive the papal blessing that put me especially in mind of Rome and of a pilgrimage made to that Eternal City during the mid 1920's by my mother, father and self. It was part of the parental scheme for my educational and spiritual improvement that, if possible, we achieve the privilege of having an audience with the Pope. None of us knew exactly how to go about getting it for we were not of the Faith. It would have been difficult to define just what the family faith was. Mother, baptized a Catholic, but for some reason not brought up as one, wavered between the Episcopal Church "because such nice people went there" and Ethical Culture "because of that wonderful Dr. Adler"; Father, although he was the son of a Universalist preacher, adapted himself with an actor's sense of theatre to whatever church, temple or even mosque in which he chanced to find himself . . . not that he very often did; while I, being at the time desperately in love with an actor who was an ardent Christian Scientist, was temporarily immersed in Mary Baker Eddy. My father, through his friends in the Catholic Actor's Guild was able to pull a few ecclesiastical wires and we ended up with an official letter introducing the Skinner family to the head of the American College of Priests in Rome. The fact that the letter was from Cardinal Hayes awed us all very much. Mother put it, for safekeeping, along with our passports, which

44

meant that it got lost quite often as Mother, with her sense of infinite variety was always finding new places where our passports could be successfully hidden from everybody, including herself. The final place she had picked out had been the bottom of my overnight case in which a bottle of Chanel's Gardenia had come unstoppered, and when we unearthed the precious document, it reeked less of the odor of sanctity than of the sort of sachet you send your cousin at Christmas. Our stay in Rome being limited, we were due to deliver the letter that afternoon. We aired it out as best we could and by the time we drove up to the doors of the American College Mother optimistically concluded that whoever read it would think it was incense. A handsome monsignor received us with cordial dignity, read the pungent communication without either batting an eyelid or dilating a nostril and told us he would be most happy to arrange for an audience . . . it might take a few days . . . he could not say how many . . . but in due course we would receive our formal invitation from the Vatican. Father thanked him, so did Mother, then added with a distressed flutter, "I think your Reverence should know that we're not Catholics" and at that we all three looked as though the old story of our each having served a jail sentence had at last caught up with us. "But," Mother added brightly, "we'd all like to be!" The monsignor smiled warmly. People always smiled warmly at Mother. However, he also rose abruptly. Possibly he figured there would hardly be time for

45

him to teach us our catechism prior to our audience. With a few kindly assurances to the effect that the papal benediction could extend even to such heretics as we, he politely saw us to the door and down the steps. We clambered into our waiting carrozza with the pious expressions of choir boys under the appraising eye of a deacon and, sitting very upright, drove back to our hotel where, with the aid of a few *americanos* sipped in the loggia to the strains of *Valencia,* we relaxed into our habitual and more secular manner.

Some two hours later while we were freshening up for dinner, there came an impressive knock on the door which I opened to admit the still more impressive presence of a gigantic individual, startlingly clad in the Michelangelo costume of the Papal Guard. At sight of this magnificent blue and white creature in striped doublet and hose I gasped, Mother uttered a breathless "My!" and Father came out with a clarion "Good God!" The dazzling giant handed Father an envelope embossed with the Vatican seal, said something about the "Papa" which, I hissed at my parent meant Pope not Poppa, bowed and departed. Father opened the envelope, took out a heavy card exquisite with engraving and Spencerian penmanship, studied it for some time then handed it to Mother with the excuse that he didn't have his glasses. Mother also studied it for a period, then looked up with the triumphant expression of someone who has just broken the enemy code and said, "Why it's perfectly simple . . . it's in Latin." Father asked her what it said if it was so simple, to which mother countered that she hadn't the slightest idea. "But," she said with maternal pride, "Cornelia's just had two years at Bryn Mawr," and she passed the card on to me. My last practice in Latin had been that of memorizing an English trot of the *Æneid*, which hadn't exactly equipped me for such social emergency as now confronted me. "This may take a little time," I said, and retired to the bedroom to do my homework, muttering over, as I went, the verbs that take the dative. Be it to the glory of Bryn Mawr that it took only some fifteen concentrated minutes for my Latin to come back to me (there wasn't much to come) and I returned to my parents with the information that our audience was set for the following morning at 11:30. This didn't give us much time in which to make our preparations, not that we knew what preparations to make. We were aware that there were strict regulations in the matter of clothes, but we were quite vague as to what they were. Mother gave a little moan and said oh dear, what a pity it was we weren't Catholics, an observation she was to repeat at periodic intervals during the ensuing twenty-four hours. We consulted the hotel manager to whom the dilemma of untutored American Protestants was an old and pretty uninteresting story. The signor, came the expressionless patter, could wear *il smoking* . . . dinnerjacket and black tie; the signora must wear all black . . . high neck, long sleeves, headcovering of a black veil; the signorina likewise . . . however, the signorina might, if

47

she chose, go in all white as she was still . . . and he coughed discreetly . . . a signorina, a blanket observation I considered highly insulting. I was going through my F. Scott Fitzgerald period and it infuriated me to be considered a virgin, especially when it was perfectly true.

After dinner we started rigging out our individual attire. Father's dinner clothes offered no problem and Mother claimed that my white tailored sports dress would do nicely augmented with a lace mantilla I had acquired (aping the one I had seen on Lila Lee). I was anything but enthusiastic about this spotless raiment and when I eventually wore it, did so with an expression that I hope implied there was more in it than met the eye. Outfitting Mother was more involved. The hotel manager had informed her that there was a shop near St. Peter's where they rented out second-hand raincoats to serve in an emergency . . . a suggestion she turned down, saying she didn't think raincoats would be reverent and besides, she whispered, they might have creatures. Mother's only black dress had a low-cut neck, elbow-length sleeves and was trimmed with a bright beaded belt which, in the grotesque fashion of the 1920's, struck her somewhere between the knees and the bottom of her round little rump. No amount of pinning would close up the space which disclosed an ample expanse of her pretty neck. Father said it must be filled in and that her sleeves too would do well with some lengthening. Mother found this last bit of advice absurdly superfluous and asked how the exposure of her forearms could possibly upset the Pope to which Father replied that he didn't know, he'd never been a Pope but the female regulations called for long sleeves and he closed the argument with the actor's phrase of last resort, "You'll have to fake it." Mother asked what with and, in a tone of finality Father answered, "Stuff."

Having on hand, of course, no vestige of "stuff," the only alternative was to go out early next morning and purchase some. Leaving Father behind with instructions to get dressed in his dinner clothes, Mother and I set out in a taxi and rode to three department stores all of which proved to be hermetically closed. The driver eventually offered the slightly belated explanation that this was Monday and that no shops opened before noon. He was quite indifferent to our distress until I explained that we were due for a papal *audienza* and that we could not possibly go unless we obtained some black material with which to fill in my mother's neck. In my halting Italian I think I said "with which to stuff down my mother's throat" but he got the idea and was instantly all helpfulness. He had a friend in the Jewish quarter, he said, the shops there were open and he drove us to the establishment of an amiable little orthodox merchant who obligingly supplied us with two yards of nun's veiling. Halfway back to the hotel, Mother suddenly remembered her Catholic acquaintances whose numbers were legion and who, she said, would be hurt if she didn't bring them all rosaries . . . to be sure they probably al-

ready had more than they knew what to do with, still
they might welcome a few freshly blessed ones, and
she stopped the taxi by a catchpenny pavement booth
and amid the conglomeration of mosaic pins, and ala-
baster reproductions of Cupid and Psyche, was able
to extricate some two dozen rosaries which the vendor,
deaf to our protests that we were in a hurry and didn't
want them wrapped, insisted upon doing up, each in
a little twist of brownish tissue paper, like salt water
taffies.

By the time we returned to our rooms it was after
ten-thirty. Father, still in drawers and undershirt, was
postponing until the last possible moment the embarrassment of putting on a dinner jacket at such a peculiar hour. Mother panted at him for heaven's sake
to hurry and get into his clothes at the same time as
she hurried to get out of hers. She had yet to remodel
her black dress. With a scant half hour to go, the only
expedient was for her to put it on and stand while
I sewed in the necessary modesties. Dressmaking was
not, along with Latin, one of the equipments for life
Bryn Mawr had given me. However, I went to work
as best I could, hardly assisted by Mother's inability
to remain stationary. The chief cause of her fidgeting
was Father who was still wandering about in a state
of unhappiness and semi-nudity. It seemed he could
not locate his studs. Mother suggested a list of likely
and unlikely places and in the end he had to resort to
a couple of brass clips pried from the manuscript of
his next season's play. Mother thought this somewhat

profane but Father said not at all; it might prove very auspicious.

By dint of some rather cavalier basting and folding under of raw edges, I managed to change Mother's shameless neckline into a demure dickey. My reformation of the forearms was less chic, being some floating attachments that looked like dangling lining. However, we felt sanguine that she would pass the papal censor except, perhaps, in the matter of the belt of colored beadwork. This was firmly attached to the dress. It seemed a pity to rip it off. On the other hand, it would be a greater pity if, because of such profane frippery she were to be barred from entrance. She decided to leave the belt as it was but also, "just in case," she'd carry along some scissors. It was Father who did the carrying . . . the only available scissors being a shearlike pair too large for her handbag. Father patiently stuck them in his dinner jacket pocket where they clanked musically against his loose change.

Minutes were fleeting and I had still a few gaps to stitch up. Mother for some time had been urging Father to go down and procure us a carrozza . . . a taxi, she felt, would not be sufficiently reverent; and Father kept finding excuses to putter about the room. Finally, mustering her utmost in vehemence she turned on him and wailed in a fluting tremolo, "Otis, why *don't* you go down and get us a carrozza?"

"If you must know, Maud," my Father snapped, "I'm afraid someone'll mistake me for a waiter!" and he strode from the room. I finished sewing Mother in for the duration, we adjusted our respective veils and hastened down to a waiting open carriage in which was sitting my father, looking uncomfortable and remarkably like a waiter. His appearance was further complicated by the fact that he was wearing a pair of black cotton gloves. Mother, at sight of them, emitted a shrill of hysteria and asked what they were for and where he had ever gotten them. He replied that they were for the Pope and that he'd gotten them back in 1919 when he had served as a pallbearer in the funeral of a theatrical manager. Mother's mirth must have weakened his confidence in them for he took them off, with injured dignity and stuffed them in his pocket along with the scissors. We gave our imposing address to the driver who, upon hearing it, paid tribute to the solemnity of the occasion by whipping up his horse and bolting us down the Corso and over the Tiber with the speed of a bat out of hell. Still clinging to the armrests of the careening vehicle, we came to a stop with a violent jerk before the indicated Vatican doors. Two gorgeous guards admitted us and turned us over to a third who led us through a labyrinth of marble corridors. Mother began making the little cooing noises she emitted whenever she felt that Father and I were about to do something that would shame us all. She repeated her comment about oh, dear, what a pity it was we weren't Catholic. Then she remembered her collection of rosaries and started taking them out of her bag. They were still done up in the salt water taffy twists. Feeling that this covering might insulate the beads against proper blessing,

52

she carefully undid each one and hung it on her arm. Then, there being no wastebaskets around the Vatican, the question arose of how to dispose of the pieces of paper. Mother solved it by doing them up into two puffy wads which she handed to Father with a bland, "Here, dear love." Father, with the expression of an early Christian martyr, jammed them into his pockets along with the shears and the black cotton gloves. His dinner jacket was beginning to take on the appearance of saddlebags.

Our letter from Cardinal Hayes had gained us the special distinction of a semi-private audience, separate from the larger devotional crowd, in a small salon, the only other occupants of which were two very lovely looking nuns, obviously persons of considerable ecclesiastical importance. Mother whispered that they were Mother Superiors (one wondered how she knew) and that we must watch them closely and do whatever they did. It didn't seem too practical a suggestion as that moment both were engaged in intent perusals of their prayer-books and we didn't even have a Baedecker among us. Mother compromised by folding her hands before her and staring at them with pious concentration. This embarrassed Father who put on his reading glasses and walked about the room, examining the pictures in a manner of self-conscious Protestant indifference, which in turn embarrassed me. I stood apart, pretending I didn't know either of them very well. We had not long to wait before a uniformed official appeared, bearing a sort of Malvolio staff, hastily herded us into a row and told us to get onto our knees. Somehow, in the confusion, the Skinners got separated so that the final line-up, reading from right to left, turned out to be first Father then a nun, then myself, then the other nun and finally mother, looking more nunlike than the authentic ones. The doors at the right opened to admit the truly impressive entrance of the Pope, wonderfully magnificent in white. He took us in with a brief glance, gave what I presume was a general blessing, then approached us individually, beginning with Father who, I was shamed to note, received his benediction with head not bowed in piety but raised in an attitude of attention that was at least dutiful. I was further mortified to note that when His Holiness extended the great ring, my parent, instead of kissing it, politely shook hands. The next blessing recipient was one of the Mother Superiors who, with beautiful grace, reached for the gloved finger tip, kissed the ring, crossed herself and made appropriate response in devotional Latin. It then being my turn, I tried to do as she had done, but in my nervousness, I must have clutched the papal hand too intensely for just as I was about to kiss the ring it was yanked away and the heavy jewel came in contact with an upper tooth from which it excised a neat chip. Horrifying as this was, I did not feel that "I *beg* your pardon!" was the thing to say at the moment; nor did I think it would be seemly to scramble forth and try to salvage the piece of tooth. I let it go as an act of penance. The Pontiff went on with some haste to the second nun who reacted with the same exquisite dedication as her fellow sister. He then paused before Mother. She kissed the ring most charmingly, crossed herself and lifted her head in the manner of St. Cecelia having a particularly good vision. The Pope spoke his words of benediction and to my amazement I heard Mother responding with a stream of little unintelligible sounds . . . not words exactly, just low musical syllables. I thought perhaps that the awesomeness of the ceremony had overworked her volatile emotions and that she had temporarily gone a bit daft. However, the Pope did not appear to think so. He paused, listened, smiled and gave her an additional blessing before continuing on to other devotees in the adjoining room.

As soon as we got outside I asked my mother what on earth it was she had said in her response. "Nothing," she answered. "It was just because I was so ashamed of us all. There were those two nuns looking so lovely and saying such beautiful things in Latin and we Skinners looking so hick and saying nothing, so I decided to make noises that sounded like Latin . . . and if the Pope didn't understand, he'd put it down to an American accent. But I think he understood." And the curious thing is, I believe he did.

Laugh Happy

A SMART, INTELLIGENT WOMAN OF THE WORLD

Laugh Happy

he phenomenon of laughter is periodically being explained in those analytical books which publishers feel they must from time to time bring out for reasons difficult to fathom unless it be for purposes of reducing a portion of the reading public to a state of glum sobriety. Not being a member of that particular portion of the reading public, I wouldn't know whether or not they treat upon one inexplicable phase of human hilarity that has frequently baffled me . . . namely, what it is that causes certain perfectly normal people, when they find themselves in certain perfectly normal situations, to go in for perfectly abnormal laughter. By perfectly normal people, I mean persons of education and poise and, furthermore, persons who ordinarily possess an averagely good sense of humor.

What, for example, prompts women who once went to school together, to yell with maniacal mirth when they meet after an interval of years that is, God knows, no laughing matter. They don't even have to have been particularly close friends for the reaction of even the most dignified matron to be one of wild vocal glee.

One of my best friends (and some of my best friends *are* friends) does it on the telephone. When she was last staying with me, she had occasion, in regard to a college fund drive, to call up a number of former New York classmates, most of whom she had scarcely seen since Daisy-chain Day. My friend is a smart, intelligent woman of the world and so, to the best of my knowledge, are her old acquaintances and yet their behavior was on a par with that of a teen-ager witnessing an antic of Danny Kaye. Possibly it was the sudden sound of theirs and my friend's maiden sobriquets that produced the same curious effect upon them all. "Hello, Gussie Adams?" . . . or . . . "Happy Cooley?" my friend would say in, I'm afraid, somewhat of a don't-open-till-Christmas tone . . . "Well, this is Bobbie Parker." There would follow a moment of stunned silence broken by a pretty rapturous, "Yes, it really is!" from my friend and then an explosion of mad laughter from her and, distinctly audible through the receiver, equally mad laughter from Gussie Adams or Happy Cooley . . . which, needless to say, died rather abruptly as soon as the subject of a donation to the college fund was broached.

In all due loyalty to my sex (a loyalty which incidentally, I don't particularly harbor) I am brash enough to assert that this sort of foundationless mirth is by no means a feminine manifestation. Groups of men, under special circumstances, are prone to similarly hysterical behavior. Among the special circumstances one does not, of course, include conventions . . . masculine behavior on such occasions being reduced to a status which it is best not to think about. But take, for example, that small group of die-hards who are conceded, chiefly by themselves, to be the pillars of an affluent and socially prominent men's club . . . the sort who have converted the old school tie into the Brooks Brothers hatband, who still believe in Landon for President and who think that Van Johnson is something turned out by General Motors. Not, I make haste to record, that I speak from any first-hand knowledge, for I have never crashed such sanctified lodges even on Ladies' Day. My information has been gleaned from one or two observant gentlemen friends who tell me they derive a fair amount of diversion studying the behavior of their fellow members . . . particularly their behavior in the club bar. For it would seem to be a matter of unwavering precedent that the bar must be the setting for side-splitting outbursts of an amicably derisive nature in the relationship of its patrons one with another. The unwritten but understood house-rule is that everybody regard everybody else as a potential and colossal joke, a joke which is extremely hard to explain. It does

61

not necessarily stem from an intake of alcohol, nor is it, God knows, due to nervous shyness. No one has to do or say anything particularly funny. No one even has to come out with a new joke concerning whoever is running on the Democratic ticket. The only requirement is for a member to walk into the bar and be seen by a group of his friends who have previously assembled there. Let us say that a hypothetical Mr. Botts happens to drift in from his office for a five-o'clock martini. Mr. Botts is a worthy citizen, perfectly average and averagely perfect. Mr. Botts' aspect is that of any well-behaved, successful business man. There is nothing that appears to be in the least funny about Mr. Botts . . . nothing in the least ludicrous. In fact, the average female, finding herself placed next to Mr. Botts at dinner, would be hard put to it to discover anything faintly amusing about him. And yet, the minute Mr. Botts makes his dignified entrance through the walnut archway, his reception by whoever of his acquaintances are already foregathered, is one of instantaneous hilarity. The club being the sort it is, the hilarity is perforce of a decidedly well-bred nature, slightly muffled but none the less explosive. "Why there's Botts!" someone exclaims. "Not *Botts!*" another replies in a tone of glad incredulity while a third halloos an antiphonal "Well I'll be doggoned . . . *Botts!*" The mere repetition of the name seems to be excruciating. There then follows a good-natured torrent of speculations, comments and interrogations, any one of which is quite a panic to its author. "Lay

you odds ten to one he orders a martini." (Laughter.)
"Well, naturally he'll order a martini." (More laughter.) "Listen, Botts without a martini is like a wedding
without a bride." (Hearty guffaws.) "Hey, Bottsy-
boy! What's to prevent you using this chair here?"
(This also is pretty delicious.) Bottsy-boy turns, sees
his friends and approaches them in a manner which
is completely normal but which, unaccountably, calls
for a fresh outburst of glee in which Mr. Botts, also
unaccountably, joins. "Botts, you old crook, how's
your behavior?" This quite convulses everybody as
does Mr. Botts' reply to the effect that he guesses his
behavior is just about as crooked as usual. There follow some lively variations on the theme of Botts . . .
Botts the good egg, Botts the martini king, Botts the
old blister . . . etc., etc., to which Mr. Botts responds
in an equally lively counterpoint of comments about
his associates, each side exhibiting a jocose appreciation of the other, the nature of which, if incomprehensible, is at least huge. After which, one must in all
charity presume, the conversation settles down to flow
in more sober channels.

One of the most productive milieus for such inex-
plicable mirth is the daily radio woman's program:
the sort conducted by a genial lady . . . let us call
her Sally Lunn . . . who talks to the housewives of
America about books, soapflakes, plays, movies, worthy causes and chocolate-mix. Helping her out in the
way of a determinedly informal stooge is some young
man with a name like Dave, whose job it is to catch

the conversational bones tossed him by Miss Lunn
and to reply with a tooth-flashing "yes *indeed*" to such
questions as doesn't he think that the girl who can
turn out that flaky, crunchy, feathery piecrust knows
the right answer to what Mr. Average Man wants?
Dave is usually quite a glamor lad who looks as though
he expected a girl to produce something more than
a piecrust, however feathery, crunchy or flaky. Never-
theless, he responds to Sally Lunn's every observation
with a boyish zest that is most disarming, particularly
so to the select little studio audience composed of
feminine devotees of the program who flock in from
Queens and Hackensack to receive from Sally Lunn's
own lips the latest household hint which is less a hint
than a product plug in the form of a positive threat.
In addition to Dave, who is a regular fixture, there is
frequently a "distinguished guest" who, in compliance
with the folksy informality of the program "has just
happened to drop by the studio and it's certainly going
to be a big surprise when you hear who it is." It's no
surprise to the guest who is usually the author of a
recently published book or a member of the cast of a
newly produced play and whose just happening to
drop by the studio has been effected at the point of
a gun by the publishers' or management's press agent.
Every once in a while I find myself placed in the position of having to drop by a studio for one of these
cheery and heavily sponsored back-fence chats and
I admit I have always honestly enjoyed them.

There stands out in my mind a particular occasion

in a large Midwestern city when the local Miss Lunn had me . . . if I may be forgiven the obstetrical verbiage . . . on her program. She, like all the other Miss Lunns, was an affable lady whose fireside manner of talking was a cozy smoke screen to the fact that she was as bright as a new silver dollar and up on more things than chocolate-mix. She too employed a tooth-flashing Dave and to her too flocked a studio audience of devoted housewives. That day it was composed of an out-of-town bridge and needlework club who called themselves something like the Busy Bees of Upper Gritville. Attendance at a Sally Lunn broadcast was apparently part of their annual outing. They all nursed a great many parcels on their bodily portions that had once been laps, all had flower-trimmed hats perched above rigid little wave-sets and every last one of them wore glasses of either the hex- or octagonal type. Miss Lunn greeted them as old friends and started off her program with a few warming up exercises. In a brisk, vitamin-enriched voice, she asked how many of the ladies had tried out that biscuit recipe she'd talked about last Thursday . . . at which there was practically a unanimous showing of hands. Miss Lunn made a feint to count the hands, gave up after fourteen in pretty confusion and said, "My, Dave! Isn't that just wonderful?" and Dave replied "It sure is, Sally," and at that, everybody laughed. Miss Lunn then switched from baking-powder to the cinema and inquired of the Busy Bees how many of them had seen a certain current picture. Again there

was a goodly showing of hands upon which Miss Lunn
again made laudatory comment to Dave who responded with an enthusiastic "Yes, indeedy," and
again they all laughed. The picture, it seemed, was a
technicolor vehicle for a starlet whose lovely peaches-
and-cream complexion put Miss Lunn in mind of that
new dairy product everybody was raving about . . .
if not everybody, she at any rate did for quite a time.
Then, after a brief pause for reading a letter from a
faithful listener in East Zenith and for extending birth-
day greetings to another in Outer Horizon, Miss Lunn
turned her attention to me. I had been sitting in a
somewhat tentative manner between herself and
Dave, taking no part in the proceedings other than
to bare my teeth in periodic attempts to show my willingness to join in the general fun. Miss Lunn now
brought me forth as something in the nature of a great
big tomato surprise. How many of the ladies, she inquired, had seen Miss Skinner in her play? This time,
the showing of hands was so negligible, Miss Lunn
didn't pause to make comment and Dave, perfect
gent that he was, didn't look. Miss Lunn, with speedy
tact, went on to say that she herself was just crazy
about the show, that the sets were just perfect and
the costumes were just . . . well, out of this world
. . . which sounded a trifle alarming. This gratuitous
information her audience received in polite silence
until she added that the play was a very, very enter-
taining comedy and at that they all laughed. The next
few minutes were devoted to an interview with me

and a few pleasant plugs for our attraction, which must have sounded like a Beethoven symphony to the ears of the press agent if he was tuned in. It was all purely routine. Miss Lunn's questions were not in the least bantering or even coy. Furthermore, I was suffering from a wretched head cold and my comebacks were of anything but a sparkling nature; and yet, due perhaps to Miss Lunn's utterance of the word comedy or of her announcement of the fact that I had once written a humorous book, our conversation was regarded in the light of a Burns and Allen routine. The dialogue went something like this:

Miss Lunn: Miss Skinner, Dave and I both saw your
   play, didn't we, Dave?
Dave: I'll say we did, Sally. (*Friendly grin from Dave,
   motherly smile from Sally, modest smirk from
   me and beams of pleasure flashing through the
   hexagonal glasses of the Busy Bees.*)
Miss Lunn: Well do tell us, Miss Skinner, how on earth
   you manage to move around the stage in all those
   heavy trains and things?
Me: Oh, you get used to them like anything else.
Miss Lunn: I don't believe *I* ever would.
Me: You can't tell. (*Sudden laughter from everyone
   in which I join nervously until the realization that
   it is in appreciation of my wit cuts me off short.*)
Miss Lunn: Tell us, Miss Skinner, just between ourselves (*and, one assumed, her million-odd listeners*), do you ever get stage fright?

67

Me: Ever? Practically constantly. (*A bare statement of fact which is taken as a gag.*)

After some further chit-chat in regard to the drama, Miss Lunn turns into more personal channels.

Miss Lunn: I know our listeners would just love to know something about your private life, Miss Skinner.

Me: (*bravely*) What would you like to know, Miss Lunn?

Miss Lunn: You're married, aren't you?

Me: Yes. (*This confession is met with a titter and a few clucking noises from the studio audience which I choose to interpret as sounds of approval.*)

Miss Lunn: And you have a son, haven't you?

Me: Yes. (*More titters and clucking noises.*)

Miss Lunn: How old is he?

Me: Seventeen. (*This gets a big laugh. It is topped by one that follows shortly afterward when, due to the exigencies of my cold, I am forced to blow my nose, a homely act that quite slays them.*)

And thus, more or less, it continued during our question and answer period which, at a given signal from the control room relayed by Dave in a sort of suave frat-sign, terminated with an abrupt "Thank you, Miss Skinner, for dropping in today" from Sally, accompanied by a friendly but definite wave of dismissal. I rose and after a perfunctory flurry of gloved applause made an unobtrusive getaway, leaving Miss Lunn extolling the excellence of Ma Somebody's Kitchen Kandies while Dave uttered yum-yum noises and the Busy Bees laughed riotously. I dashed for the nearest elevator. I felt frazzled and foolish. My facial muscles were aching and the prospect of ever smiling again was like the prospect of ever taking a drink again for someone suffering from a severe hang-over. In the elevator my tension started to ease; all the occupants seemed solemn and the operator had a balefully preoccupied manner. Once outside, things took on a more cheerful aspect; the sky was gray and lowering, the streets were crowded with frantic, scuttling people. They all had serious expressions and a few looked downright disagreeable. Two taxis clashed fenders and the language that poured from the mouths of their respective drivers was colorfully Homeric. A fat woman in a mink coat collided with my left elbow and snarled something to the effect that persons who didn't look where they were going ought to be shot. I snarled back something to the effect that some persons ought to try dropping dead and went on my way with a lighter tread. It seemed a good life, after all.

Bag of Bones

MY SON LOOKED DEFINITELY AWED

Bag of Bones

e came across the bones on a Colorado Rocky Mountain a few yards below timber line. It was my ten-year-old son who spied them. He was riding ahead of the cowboy and me, and, at the curve in the trail which projected giddily above a drop of several hundred feet, he reined in his horse and called out, "Look! Dinosaur bones!" as casually as one might have announced the discovery of an old beer bottle. He was pointing at something on the other side of the trail and there, a little way out in a boulder field were indeed some very large and very gray bones. We all three dismounted and scrambled over the intervening rocks, my child and I having a heated discussion because I said they couldn't be dinosaur bones and he asked why they

couldn't be and I said because dinosaur bones were
so large museums had to add on sort of hangars to
house them, which he said didn't prove anything
because these might be just its toes and I said well
they weren't, and he said how did I know they
weren't and by that time we had reached them.
There were four in all, about the length and thickness
of good-sized firelogs, with curious nubbly ends.
Weathered to a point of seeming partially petrified,
they looked strange and, I had to admit, very ancient.
My son's eyes opened wide like camera lenses and his
reaction, I'm sorry to say, was to whoop, "Maybe I
can sell them to the Natural History Museum!" We
stared at them in speculation. I had no idea what they
were and even the cowboy said he was dogged if he
knew although they might have once belonged to a
buffalo. My child, who has definitely ghoulish tenden-
cies, was charmed with them and announced that
since he had discovered them, he "fenned" for them
—a claim which was set up undisputed. When it
came to taking them back with us then and there,
however, I demurred. But he begged, demanded and
"Oh-pleased" with such fervor, I gave in and the
three of us dragged and bumped the great unwieldy
objects back to the horses who weren't any too glad
to see them. We managed to hoist and lash each onto
the back of a saddle, while the long-suffering cowboy
carried the fourth in front of him like a mace. Despite
some slight resentment on the part of the horses, we
got them back to the ranch where my son added relish

74

to the evening meal by making a tour of the dining room and asking the other boarders what they thought they were. The fact that nobody seemed to know added appreciably to their value. He lugged them back to our cabin and arranged them on the stone mantelpiece where they remained as a tasty decoration for the remainder of our sojourn in Colorado.

The eve of our departure was attended by the usual packing hysteria. I thought we had brought along sufficient luggage, but my son's violent appreciation of the West had expressed itself by going in lavishly for local purchases in the way of western boots, ten-gallon hats, studded belts and a number of further things that won't pack. I had reached the state when, whimpering with rage and frustration, I was alternately tramping about on a bursting duffel bag and thumping myself with mighty impacts of my rear on a suitcase which refused to shut, in the midst of which crisis, my little boy came beaming into the room, cheerfully courting annihilation. It was his fourth appearance that evening. Each time he had brought me objects of unpackable proportions and each time I had bellowed at him to get out and stay out. He now arrived empty-handed, but he pointed to the macabre display above the mantelpiece and said sweetly, "Don't forget, Mummy. I'm taking those with me." With heroic forbearance, I conquered an impulse to hurl a bootjack at him and asked icily just what he imagined they'd go in. He looked at the various over-

flowing receptacles and at my expression and said,
"Oh," so meekly, I softened and told him he might
take his trophies with him if he'd get them tied up in
a package and he went off to the main house, happily
staggering and lurching beneath the load. He prevailed upon our waitress to do up the bundle for him.
Our waitress was a student from Teacher's State and
everyone agreed she was a lovely girl, but her talent
for tying up bundles was on a par with her talent
for waiting, which was negligible. She wrapped the
osseous specimens in pieces of shelf paper and tied it
all up with yards of white cotton string, the sort they
put around light parcels in drygoods stores. It was
massive and bulky and due to the inadequate string,
the only way to carry it was by both arms, in a hug-
ging fashion. It weighed around forty pounds.

Our jumble of luggage looked disreputable enough
as it was, and the addition of this gem didn't lend it
any too much tone. Nor were we ourselves particularly in keeping with the swank atmosphere of the
streamlined train we were taking. Our traveling
clothes, which for two months had been rammed into
a small closet behind an accumulation of bluejeans
and other rugged apparel, lacked something of their
original smartness. My hat had not only lost its shape,
it had taken on a curious new one, while the one my
child had worn on the outward trip had completely
disappeared, a loss which delighted him because it
meant he could wear his Tom Mix model, and that
certainly contrasted quaintly with his best Brooks

Brothers suit. His head, under the clippers of the local barber, had been glorified with a haircut which left it looking like plush in back and heavy thatch in the front. My complexion which, out on the Range I had secretly admired as being glowing and rather radiant, with the addition of city make-up and hair-do, looked like Sadie Thompson's. My vanity suffered a further blow by the realization that my nose was peeling.

The porter, used to the more expensive dude ranch trade, greeted us politely, but without much warmth. His enthusiasm waned even more when, upon being asked if he could find a place in which to stow the great unwieldy bundle, he picked it up by the string which instantly snapped, as a layer of paper burst asunder and an ancient femur clattered down onto the Burlington's best deluxe carpet.

Laughing nervously, I explained, "It's just some bones, ha! ha! . . . my little boy found. We're taking them back with us, ha-ha! . . . because we don't know what they are."

The porter's expression was one which indicated he wasn't far from guessing they were human and might still have traces of recently murdered flesh on them. I felt rather flustered. My ten-year-old, however, was quite unconcerned. His was the objective attitude of the scientist. Upon arrival in New York he planned to go directly to the Museum of Natural History where the bones could be analyzed and valued. After which, he said he might consider selling them, provided, of course, he was offered a sufficiently high

77

price. Then he spent an hour or more in happy speculation over just what he would purchase with the proceeds. He began with a Sealyham terrier and ended with a Chris-Craft. His enthusiasm was contagious and I began to share a few of his illusions. Not that I foresaw any immediate ownership of a Chris-Craft, but I found myself thinking that maybe these were rare specimens after all, and in fond maternal fancy, summoned up a charming picture of a group of eminent scientists patting my son on the head, praising him in learned language and presenting him with a medal or a little citation, or even a small stuffed animal.

We reached Chicago in the morning. It was one of those days when the buildings wiggle in the heat and people with a fancy for such pastimes fry eggs on sidewalks. We had a four-hour wait-over between trains—a period I had planned to spend in the air-cooled sanctuary of some movie house. But I was reckoning without the burning scientific fervor of my offspring. He recalled the fact that Chicago was the home of the Field Museum—a flash of youthful intelligence which, at any other time, would have filled me with quiet pride. Why couldn't we take the bones over there and have them analyzed? I instantly stated every conceivable reason why we couldn't, even to that back-to-the-wall last stand argument, "Because I say so." I tried all the best established forms of bribery in the way of news reels, double-frosted-chocolate-fudge whatsies, rifle ranges and a trip up the tallest building, but my son was adamant. He even became lofty-minded, reproached me for considering trivialities at a time of such import and his final play was to point out the fact that for weeks I had been begging him to enlarge his mental interests beyond the bounds of comics and the Lone Ranger, and now that he was doing so, I was being anything but co-operative. At that I gave in. We checked the remainder of our luggage at the station, a porter heaved our massive parcel into a taxi and I gave the address to the driver.

I can't say I shared my son's happy anticipation. To be sure the idea was highly commendable. Furthermore, I told myself, what if the bones *should* turn out to be rarities? To which an inner voice answered back, what if they shouldn't?

The Field Museum is not a building around which porters loiter and, as everyone knows, the approach is up an impressively vast stairway. The taxi man made no offer to help us and I was too ashamed to ask him. There was no alternative but for us both to lug the burden between us. By now the shelf paper wrapping had split in a number of places and several yards of string had come unwound and was trailing along the ground and occasionally twining itself about our respective ankles. Some of it still remained wound about the package, but we knew if we took hold of it, it would burst, so we carried the monstrosity between us, holding up either end with both hands, which meant we had to face each other and

ascend the majestic stairs in a sideways gait. The heat
beat down in blinding intensity and the package
seemed to grow in weight. It split in a number of new
places and a protruding bone kept gouging me in the
stomach at every step. I bore up only through the
thought that it wouldn't last much longer. I am not
in the habit of taking specimens into museums and
mine was the simple notion that all one did was go
in and walk right up to the first guard who would in-
spect what one had brought and pass judgment on it
then and there. But for the benefit of any fellow layman who has recently found an old tomahawk or a
stray pterodactyl egg, I should like to state that the
procedure is far less direct.

Panting and puffing, we gained the top of the stairs
and managed somehow to get through the door. The
main hall opened out before us in all its immensity
and the colossal group of trumpeting elephants tow-
ered above us. The misgivings which had assailed me
in the taxi returned, and my son looked definitely
awed. But spurring myself on with little mental en-
couragements of the "nothing ventured, nothing
gained" variety, I approached the first uniformed man
I saw and, bright as a button, said, "How do you do!"

He grunted a cautious sort of reply and his expression indicated he expected my next move would be
to whip out an insurance policy. In a horrifyingly glad
tone I continued, "My little boy and I have some
bones here. What shall we do about them?"

"How's that?" said the guard.

"Some bones," I said. "We found some bones . . . out in Colorado, and . . ."

"*I* found them!" burst in my son, to which the guard, pretty much at sea, said, "That was fine, Sonny," with perfunctory politeness.

"We'd like to have them analyzed," I said timidly. "Maybe *you* could tell us what they are."

The guard sighed. It was clear he was used to my type. Then telling us to wait a minute, he left us standing in the entranceway. Passers-by stared at the nearby exhibits, then at us and the extraordinary looking bundle at our feet. I tried to look unconcerned but I was rapidly feeling more and more like an idiot, and from the forced leer on my son's face, it was clear his early bravado was wearing off. After several very long minutes the guard returned with a businesslike young woman who asked what she might do for me. Suppressing an impulse to say, "Show me the nearest exit," I grinned inanely and in a club woman's voice which I recognized with amazement was my own said, "How do you do! I'm Mrs. Blodget!" (I would have perished sooner than give my professional name.) Then for some reason I added, "From Long Island. And this is my son Dickie. We've found some bones."

The young woman eyed us and our bundle and said, "You'd like them passed on?"

"Yes," I said, "but I don't want to bother anyone. I just thought maybe you or one of the guards could tell us . . ."

81

"This way, please," she said and walked briskly off toward a door marked PRIVATE. My son and I hoisted our burden between us and followed, I muttering words to the effect that we hadn't expected them to go to all that trouble, to which the young woman with crisp politeness replied not at all, that was what they were there for and led us into a dignified reception room. She asked us if we minded waiting a minute and before giving us a chance to say whether or not we did, went swiftly out, closed a door and left us sitting on the edge of a formal settee. By now I had the definite foreboding that this was all a big mistake, but I smiled bravely at my son who was looking exactly the way he does in the dentist's waiting room. Neither of us spoke. After a time a door opened to admit a second businesslike young woman. We sprang to our feet, grinning vacuously, and again I heard myself saying, "How do you do? I'm Mrs. Blodget from Long Island and this is my son Dickie and we found some bones out in Colorado."

The young woman gave us a kindly smile. "You're in luck today," she said. "It just happens that Dr. X. is in the building doing some special research."

"Dr. X.?" I limply echoed the name she had uttered.

"Dr. X." she repeated his name. "He is our chief paleontologist."

"Oh," I croaked with awe.

"In fact," she went on indulgently, "he is the leading paleontologist of the country."

This bit of information frightened the living day-

82

lights out of me.

"Oh!" I said. "Dr. X. won't want to be bothered with us!"

"No matter how busy he is," she said sweetly, and started filling out a card, "Dr. X. always has time for science-lovers."

"But I'm not a science-lover!" I spluttered. "I mean to say, I just have some bones and I really don't think they're as good as all that!"

"Only last week," she went on inexorably filling out the card, "someone brought in quite an ordinary-looking bone and it proved to be that of a saber-toothed tiger. So you see, you never can tell."

"No, indeed you can't." I never spoke truer words.

The young woman handed me the card which she had filled in with bits of information about ourselves, told us to show it to any guards or attendants who questioned us, then led us around to a small, hidden elevator and told the boy to take us to the top floor. My heart sank as rapidly as we rose. Our parcel of bones by now looked more disreputable than ever. My hat had slipped to the back of my head, a stray wisp of hair had fallen across my face and had caught in the corner of my mouth and I was perfectly certain my nose was gleaming. I had no free hand with which to neat myself up and I was too impressed with the surrounding learned atmosphere to pause for any such worldly frivolity as adjusting my powder and lipstick.

The top floor appeared to be almost entirely roofed

in glass. The sun of that blistering day beat down upon it and we advanced, feeling like a couple of mushrooms "sous cloc he." I gasped out amazement that Dr. X. could do any research in such intense heat, to which my son (who had no more heard of Dr. X. than had I) explained, "It's probably his training in the jungle."

A guard waylaid us, read our card, and telling us to come right that way, led us to a door marked with Dr. X.'s name. Since the day in Freshman year when I was called up by the dean, I had never known such abject panic. My impulse was to turn tail and run, leaving the bundle like a foundling on Dr. X.'s doorstep. But that would have been to lose face with my son—not that mine at the moment was much of a face to lose. I took a deep breath and knocked. A mild voice said, "Come in," and with our package bumping and thudding between us, we entered the sanctum sanctorum.

Dr. X., a quiet, kindly looking gentleman, was bent over a table, gazing at something through a magnifying glass. He looked up, smiled charmingly and said, "How do you do," so pleasantly it completely disarmed me and for the third time I heard myself burbling the ghastly patter about being Mrs. Blodget, from Long Island.

He listened politely, then asked if we'd please undo our parcel. Our parcel had by now just about undone itself. With a nervous titter I struggled to disengage the snarled-up string, removed the battered bits of shelf paper and revealed our treasure. As Dr. X. gazed at them I waited for a happy gleam of recognition to light up his countenance but none lit. After a pause he looked up.

"Yes," he said, "those are the bones of a horse."

"A horse?" we echoed in weak unison.

"A horse," he repeated.

My son's face had fallen several feet. "But they're such big bones," he said.

"That's because it was a big horse," said Dr. X. There was a strained silence. Then my child, with a renewed flicker of hope, asked, "How old would you say they were?" I knew that he was hoping they dated somewhere around the Ice Age.

The eminent scientist turned one over thoughtfully and said, "About twenty-five years."

I tried to laugh off the awkward pause, burbling some inanity to the effect that I guessed he'd been bothered before by other foolish laymen, to which Dr. X. offered no reply but showed us, by way of solace, the saber-toothed tiger's bone. It looked to me a good deal like an everyday drumstick, except that it was the color of mahogany, but we gazed at it with proper expressions of awe, after which it was apparent our interview was at an end. It was also apparent that Dr. X. expected us to take our bones away with us. I cast a surreptitious glance about the room, hoping to find a large receptacle for the dumping of rejected specimens, but I failed to see even a scrap-basket. My son and I wrapped them up again in the fragments of shelf paper and rewound the bundle with the cobweb string. I spluttered some apologetic thanks and bowed and Dr. X. said, "Not at all," and also bowed. Silent and subdued, we made our way along the simmering corridor and into the elevator. We passed the guards with averted eyes and somehow managed to get out of the building and into a taxi. We didn't say much on our way to the station, nor were we especially animated during the remainder of our journey. My child, however, with a curious loyalty, still insisted upon taking the bones home with us.

There, with the aid of some crankcase oil, he stained them a deep brown and in open defiance of Dr. X. he exhibits them to his friends as part of the wing structure of a ichthyosaurus. I, for one, wouldn't dream of contradicting him.

Button, Button

MIGHT KEEP IT IN THE REFRIGERATOR

Button, Button

he approach of the Easter of 1945 and the releasing of my son from his then school started me wondering what happy surprises lie in store for me. His previous vacation, his homecoming was heralded by a letter announcing the tidings that there would arrive from a biological supply company a C.O.D. package containing an embalmed cat; that he was planning to spend his free time dissecting it; that I could count it as part of his Christmas present and, if I had no better place to store it, I might keep it in the family refrigerator. The shock to my sensibilities was somewhat tempered by the solacing thought that perhaps this macabre harbinger might be an indication of his eventually becoming an eminent surgeon. That he might, by the same token, become an eminent mortician didn't occur to me. Neither did it occur to me that once having embarked upon this particular form of holiday pursuit, he'd want to yield to any distractions of a social nature. Hitherto, parties have meant little in his life. However, having now attained the worldly age of fifteen, my son has become the recipient of a flood of invitations to attend certain organized dances that come under the heading of "Junior," which is a polite way of indicating that along with a boy's acceptance must go a parent's check, for these festivities are subscription affairs, the expenses being shouldered by the youthful participants, a worthy manifestation in these troubled times. The invitations arrived while my offspring was away at school, and, under the influence of that manly remoteness, he flatly turned down the proffered frivolity. However, as the holidays approached, learning that some of his pals were going, he changed his mind and grudgingly admitted he might go to two—"just to find out," which sounded significant.

The fact that he'd have to have a dinner jacket for these galas didn't occur to me until I overheard a fellow mother bewailing the fact that she'd been all over town to get her Oswald some tux and there wasn't a pair, or a set (or maybe it was a brace) to be had. This piece of information I found peculiarly upsetting. The idea of my child in evening clothes seemed fantastic to me who still harbors a tendency to dress him in gray shorts and Basque jumpers. Be-

sides, in my day, which I am increasingly made to
feel was contemporary with the initial publication of
"Little Women," boys attended our young fry dances
in nothing more formal than white flannels and navy
blazers in summer, and, in winter, dark blue suits and
stiff collars . . . the last item under protest. But that
was provincial suburbia then and this was Manhattan
New York now, and, as my family so often and en-
dearingly point out, I just don't know. It all struck
me as very foolish and shockingly extravagant. My son
at that period was growing with a nonstop rapidity
akin to the growth of Alice after she consumed the "Eat
Me" cake. The expenditure entailed in the purchase of
a suit he would wear only twice and then completely
outbourgeon went violently against the grain which
in me is a cautious blend of Missouri and Vermont. A
hand-me-down, I determined, was what he'd wear
and like it. The problem was to find a hander-downer.
I called up a number of acquaintances with older sons
and some whose boys were still in service. They each
gave the same discouraging response. They were
sorry but Junior's dinner clothes had already been
handed down to the little Whooziz youth. To the
horrified amazement of my more fastidious friends, I
resorted to a few of those rental houses which special-
ize in chauffeurs' and butlers' uniforms and tried to
hire a suit. In one I might have procured a full dress
white-tie-and-tail arrangement and in another I hesi-
tated over a waiter's outfit, but all dinner clothes had
been previously bespoken. As the proprietor of one of

the establishments explained, "All my regular customers are having weddings this season." Stifling my
scruples of frugality, I set out to buy a suit, a search
that dragged me through all the leading emporiums
of the city. Finally, after several days, I found one in
an emporium that wasn't especially leading and my
resentment of this enforced expenditure was somewhat mitigated by the fact that the garments were
reduced in price, the jacket having a flaw at the elbow, a locale in which every jacket springs a flaw ten
minutes after my boy has put it on anyway. Also,
being fortunate in the lack of his presence, which
would otherwise have shamed me into getting a size
that fitted, I was able to make off with one I imagine
may come in handy when he's a man of fifty. The
purchase of the tie, suspenders and collar was com-
paratively easy, but the difficulty in locating a dress
shirt in those days appeared to be as hopeless a quest as
that of tracking down a dozen nylons. The only things
to be found were soft ones and I was about to write
Lucius Beebe, requesting him to make a statement that
this season the evening attire of well-dressed youth
will be a combination of tuxedo and colored sports
shirt, when my husband's secretary, one of those treas-
ures who in every dire emergency "knows someone
downtown," was able to obtain a boiled one through
some mysterious friend who works for a stockbroker.
How she wangled it I never inquired. Had it been
handed me warm from the freshly slain body of the
stockbroker, I would have accepted it thankfully. My

son was outfitted for his first formal party and that was all I cared about.

The lad arrived from school and so, eventually, did the evening of the dance. It was scheduled to begin promptly at eight. There was a slight error in the matter of starting him dressing, owing to the fact that in the afternoon we had gone to see "The Lost Weekend," which terrifying and moral warning had so unnerved me, I had had to rush from the theatre to the house of some friends for a double Martini just to reassure myself of my sterling lack of dependence on stimulants, while my child eyed me speculatively over a Pepsi-Cola. This respite, while emotionally restorative, delayed us overtime. Pouring rain and the prevailing obsolescence of taxis forced us into an elbow-gouged journey home on the B.M.T. and we staggered in hot and gasping and ready to blame each other for things. My offspring raced upstairs for a tub and I followed in his wake. I hurried to his room and started getting out his party paraphernalia, still wearing my hat. I had forgotten about the assortment of complicated details essential to the bright evening plumage of the male. I seldom if ever have to handle these tortuosities, as my husband is blessedly the type that likes to conduct his own clothing arrangements. Reflecting in somewhat bitter retrospect on my ensuing struggles, I realized he might have been of considerable help on this occasion. But, possibly sensing trouble, he had left town for a short business trip. Perhaps it was just as well. Otherwise we would never

93

have felt so free to plunder his bureau drawers.

My son emerged from his bath bright and dripping water on a newly cleaned gray rug, brandishing my pet comb which he had clogged with vaseline for his cowlick. He removed a monogrammed linen guest towel which, for reasons known not even to himself, he had twisted into a loin cloth and announced he was ready to start. The preliminary preparations were simple, his underthings being reduced at that time to the singular in the way of a pair of shorts long since stripped of buttons whose properties for the maintenance of modesty depended upon a complicated elaboration of a bit of tape and a tie clip. When I suggested he might substitute a pair of his father's, he said emphatically no, he was used to these and anyway, since they didn't show, what was the diff. The trousers, although somewhat roomy, went on easily enough and even I know how to fasten and adjust suspenders. The sock situation was the first to offer difficulties, the collection the boy brought back from school being made up of unmated woolen sundries, lurid plaids for the most part, all marked with the name tapes of unknowns. However, he solved the problem by taking the last silk pair belonging to his father, whose feet are a good two sizes smaller, casually snipping off the toes and wearing them like mitts. Garters we ignored. I am assured that to expect the modern youth to wear garters is the equivalent of presuming a Junior Miss will appear in victorian pantalettes. Socks, I am peremptorily informed, are worn in casual folds cascading down over the shoe top with a glimpse of skin showing provocatively below the trouser bottom, and mothers just have to resign themselves to the fashion with the consolingly cultural thought that Charles the First wore his hose in somewhat the same way.

It was over the donning of the shirt that feelings on both sides started to soar. Each of us had a divergent theory as to how it went on and neither of us really knew. Discord first jangled over the question of collar buttons. Having heretofore worn only soft shirts and pullovers, my son possesses no collar buttons of his own and, in my homespun way, I was all for having him wear two modest wooden numbers that had come home in the laundry, a suggestion he took as a gross indignity. I pointed out the fact that since, like the underdrawers they didn't show, what, to use his very words, was the diff? He cast upon me the look of an offended Hapsburg prince (he can do that when his hair is faultlessly slick) and said no, nothing would do but his father's gold collar buttons. His father's gold collar buttons are kept in his top bureau drawer, not in the crest-engraved case that his son's tone implied, but in a tin Louis Sherry box along with an old watch, a nail clipper, a number of stray buttons he hopes some day I'll sew onto whatever they came off of, and a badge saying "Repeal the 18th Amendment." I don't really believe I also saw some jacks and a marble, but it's an assortment which gives that impression. The studs, on the other hand, enjoy a position of dignity in a jeweler's box that won't stay closed but is held together by a twisted Boston garter.

95

This was pounced upon by my young Brummel who announced that he guessed he'd wear the pearl dress set. I announced that I guessed he wouldn't, to which he asked why not and I answered because he'd lose them, and he inquired what made me think so; I retaliated by stating that he always lost other people's things and he asked what for instance, and I countered, well, my tennis racquet, and he said that was different as he wasn't wearing my tennis racquet. I put a stop to this spirited verbal tournament by saying bluntly that he'd wear his father's plain gold studs and like it. I was very firm. So he wore his grandfather's black onyx ones and I had to like it.

I was all for getting these somewhat idiotic gewgaws imbedded in their appointed positions before putting on the shirt, then slipping it down over the head in the manner of a turtleneck sweater. But my child said no, he would get into the shirt and I would then "stab the gadgets *on* him," which smacked somehow of primitive ceremony. He slipped on the shirt. Starting ill-advisedly enough with the neckband, I managed, with a good deal of panting, to drill the collar buttons through the areas in that solid wall of starch and goods intended to simulate apertures and on into my thumb, where they left a sizable dent and black mark. My satisfaction over this accomplishment was short-lived for it turned out I'd put the short-stemmed button where the long-stemmed one belonged and vice versa and it had to be done all over again, which made for a flurry of rancor on both sides. The second time, however, was easier, as I had wedged open the holes with a nail file and enlarged them sufficiently to permit the collar buttons not only to go on in but, at the least encouragement, to continue on out. The attachment of the collar itself we left until later. Impaling the studs in that unyielding white board jokingly known as a "bosom" offered fresh hazards. To gouge them into the front was all very well but how, I complained, to adjust that nasty little rod that has to be pulled out and released on the nether side unless you crawled under the shirt in the manner of a photographer under a black cloth. My son, by way of response, merely informed me I was dumb and while his statement contained the elements of truth, it seemed poor co-operation at the moment. I countered by saying that if it was dumbness he was looking for, he'd find it in the genus of men . . . no woman would put up with such assinine accessories; which protestations he topped by asking why, if accessories were so assinine, was I still wearing my hat. I silenced this second clash of arms by bellowing at him to hold still. By dint of tucking the end of the shirt tail under my chin and reaching up with one hand between the respective bosoms of shirt and boy, I was able to implant the studs. They showed up very nicely on the gleaming white front. So did a few impressions of my thumb.

The collar was, according to masculine standards of elegance, the exact size for the neckband, which meant it was too small for it. The back eyelet and one of the front ones connected up with a minimum of struggle, but to pull around the stiffly flighty end and

97

impale it on a wobbly button that had no firmer backing than the boy's rapidly rising larynx, required more than our combined strength. I sought help from our young cook who is the Sandow of the family and upon whom we call in all tight-lid emergencies. By means of her making a fold in the band, which was about like making a fold in a length of weather stripping, then my holding onto it with the power born of desperation while my son backed the button with his finger, the cook, pulling on the collar as if it were a stubborn saddle girth, managed to get it fastened. It was unfortunate that we'd forgotten to place the tie in it, an oversight which drove my son into a frenzied tirade in which he demanded the instant firing of his father's secretary, which hardly seemed an immediate solution. By again resorting to the nail file, I succeeded, without undoing the collar, to wedge in the tie, and the secretary's job no longer hung in the balance.

My fifteen-year-old started in on the fixing of the tie himself but gave up at the first loop and gave it over, along with his neck, to me. I am not blessed with the gift of tie tying. It impresses me as one of those smugly superfluous accomplishments like flower arranging or the ability to do up trick Christmas packages. Facing him squarely, I struggled for a time, only to effect first a bow with one side a great deal larger than the other, then a bow that looked quite lovely for a brief moment but collapsed quickly into two dangling ends. My son, whose ire had increased considerably, again informed me I was dumb. I reminded him that he was in no position to cast the first, or even the second, stone and, with injured dignity, summoned the maid and asked if she could tie a bow tie. She, also facing him, tied it, but the bow came out perpendicular, and jointly we yelled for the cook, who said she didn't know but she'd do her best. The cook's best was on a par with the maid's worst. My son, while he dearly loves them both, told them they too were dumb, a bit of gratuitous information I nervously laughed off, explaining that he would have his little joke. It is doubtful if either of them got it. This, I decided, was a crisis that called for a man, and I rang for Patrick, the elevator man. Patrick was sympathetic. He had, it seemed, worn the same tie for years, but the fact that it was made of leather and went on by means of an elastic around his neck did not make for his skill in tying a silk one. I wondered how he'd feel if I suggested borrowing his for the evening, but dismissed the idea at the thought of how my son would feel. The suggestions Patrick had to offer were well intentioned but quite useless. I thanked him and sent him back to his elevator before my son had a chance of including him in his category of the dumb. By now the wrath of that young man had assumed Homeric dimensions and the greater portion of it was aimed at me. I couldn't make out what I'd done, but decided that whatever it was I'd better do something still further. Taking my courage and the phone in hand, I rang up a kindly gentleman who lives in the next door building and asked how much he'd mind tying my boy's tie. He didn't state the amount he minded but told me pleasantly to bring the boy and tie on over. We journeyed across the way in silence, my son with his tie-ends dangling, looking very baleful indeed. The gentleman received us with charming cordiality. He led my son up to the mirror, stood directly behind him, reached both hands about his neck and, with the quiet technique of an expert, tied an elegant bow. We thanked him profusely . . . at least I did, and my man-about-town hastened off belatedly to his soiree. I returned home to supper on a tray and "Modern Man Is Obsolete." Some fortuitous inner prompting had made me feel it was wisest not to inquire when my son thought he'd be home. He returned a little before midnight and, with a tact born of instinct, I carefully disguised my relief at seeing him home safe and, to all intents and purposes, sound. In reply to my hesitant inquiry as to what the party had been like, he summed up the festivities with a descriptive "It was O.K." He did, however, pause on his way up to bed long enough to lean over my chair, give me a sound smack and say "Gee, Mom, thanks a lot."

Opening Night

STARK NAKED ON THE STAGE

Opening Night

don't know why people go on the stage. Certainly I don't know why I ever did, nor do my friends and family, who obviously regard the whole thing as a peculiar form of personal tribulation. Some weeks ago, I had an opening (the obstetrical phraseology is apposite) on Broadway, although, to judge by their behavior, it was my dear ones who underwent the more exquisite pangs.

The morning of the opening, my husband woke me by announcing in my ear that he was getting up but that he was letting me keep on sleeping. Then, in case I might have forgotten, he proffered the gratuitous reminder that I had a first night ahead of me and added the consoling information that I was to be let alone all day, completely alone. I was to take it easy. Not think about the show. Just rest. Relax. Then he lit a cigarette, inhaled and went into a choking spell, at the finish of which he asked me if I were all right. I grunted that I was and he said that was fine and he'd go away now and leave me alone. Then he walked about the room for a while. After a couple of turns, he leaned out of the window, stared down at the pavement, sniffed the air and stated in hearty tones that it was a lovely sunny day for an opening night, which didn't strike me as calling for an immediate answer. After this, he came over to the bed and remarked in tender but extremely audible tones that my covers needed fixing, yanked blanket and sheet clear off me, shook them just enough to loosen them at the foot, replaced them over me exactly as they had been before and said, "There! Isn't that better?" I again grunted in the affirmative. My husband, after once more telling me to keep on sleeping, bumped into the night table, cursed, said, "Sh!" and tiptoed out of the room.

I squinted at the clock. There were exactly twelve hours before curtain time and I figured the best way of living through them was by becoming unconscious. I was, of course, wide awake. For a fretful hour I tossed from side to side seeking oblivion, and when it finally arrived, it wasn't oblivion at all but a series of those nightmares peculiar to actors in which one finds oneself on a stage, delivering the Potion Scene stark naked to an audience of some two thousand spectators all of whom turn out to be George Jean Nathan. Again I became widely awake and began thinking about the ordeal ahead of me, or rather, continued thinking about it, for it had been my psychotic preoccupation for the past week. Lying in an attitude I chose to consider relaxed, with tense muscles, thumping heart and quavering jaw, I tried to think of other things to think about. Things that would restore my sense of values. I would put my mind on wider prospects . . . the U.N., for example. I would think about Mr. Molotov. That was difficult because I didn't know very well exactly what to think about Mr. Molotov, so I tried thinking about Mr. Byrnes and that didn't work either because it suddenly occurred to me that Mr. Byrnes bears a startling resemblance to one of the members of our cast and that got me back into the dreaded train of thought. It was no use. I rang for breakfast. My maid brought it in with the expression of a kindly neighbor bringing a floral anchor to the recently bereaved. "Tonight's the opening, isn't it?" she said in an undertone. "Aren't you nervous?" and she leered wanly in what was undoubtedly meant to be encouragement. I leered back, said, "No, not at all," slopped coffee into the saucer with one shaking hand and with the other nonchalantly picked up the morning paper. Someone had thoughtfully folded it to the theatre page and the first item to meet my eye was my own name under the foreboding heading of "Tonight's opening." This time the coffee cascaded down the front of my bed jacket. The maid, a girl of sensitive understanding, said she guessed I felt just like that poor boy Conn the morning of that fight when Joe Louis knocked him out, wistfully recalled the fact that she herself had bet on Conn and walked softly out of the room.

About this time the telephone calls commenced. The first was from my husband telling me not to talk on the telephone. I had an opening that night, I should take it easy, I must switch off the phone to everyone, just keep it open for any emergency call from him. It seemed a little involved but I said O.K. and added, "What emergency call, for instance?" He replied in the voice of Cornwallis before Yorktown, "You never know. Something may arise at the box office." I toyed with the idea of things that might arise at the box office. The way I felt, I hoped it might be one of those surprise volcanoes that recently arose in Mexico. However, I didn't enlarge upon the subject. The next call was from a friend who used to be on the stage and has since gone in for puppets. She said she saw I had an opening that night and she merely wanted to wish me Godspeed. She knew all too well what I was going through and her frank advice was never to read any notices . . . with which words of wisdom, she discreetly hung up. The bell rang again and someone said, "Hello there," this was Buzzie . . . she and George had just arrived from Duluth for their first New York spree in fifteen years, she saw I had an opening that night and how about my wangling them a couple of tickets. I explained to Buzzie, whom I vaguely recalled as having sat next to in Freshman Latin at Bryn Mawr, that what with the Guild subscription, the critics and the personal connections of the management, the only four seats I myself had been able to purchase, had gone to my husband and my three closest friends. Buzzie said, "Oh," and hung up. The next person to call up was one of my closest friends, a sportsman and a gentleman, at least I had always hitherto thought so. He too reminded me of the opening that night and he too knew what I must be going through . . . just the way he felt the morning he had to ride in the Maryland Hunt Cup steeplechase . . . time he fell at the third jump and broke his pelvis, ha-ha. It was gratifying that I knew him sufficiently well to retort that it was too bad he hadn't broken his goddam neck, ha-ha, and hang up. After that, another friend, not close, gave me a ring to let me know she was not coming to the opening but that she'd be suffering for me just the same. She had to go to a dinner party and she knew she wouldn't be able to eat a blessed thing. The next telephonic communication was from a playwright who wanted to send me a script . . . he was sure, of course, that tonight's opening would be extremely successful but, after all, it was on the knees of the gods and one never knew, did one? I agreed, somewhat wanly, that one didn't and told him to send along the script. Then my husband called and said he was in a telephone booth and I said that was nice. He wanted to know if I was taking it easy and I said sure I was and went out for a violent walk in the Park, a Turkish bath and a swim in a hotel pool.

I came home to a midafternoon meal which my

maid served in the same funereal manner in which she had brought me my breakfast, sliding softly in and out of the pantry and occasionally sighing deeply. I attempted a little casual chit-chat with her but she eyed me with an expression which indicated she knew I was only being brave and answered in monosyllables. In the middle of luncheon my husband called to ask if I were all right. He wasn't. He had terrible indigestion. He was at his club and he thought he'd just have a drink and maybe some oyster stew. I said I guessed he'd just better, too . . . which ended that conversation.

It is part of theatre tradition to spend the afternoon prior to an opening in bed, sleeping, relaxing and getting into something known as "the mood." It's a fine theory, only it never works. Sleep, if any, is fitful, relaxation is that of a prisoner waiting for the verdict and the mood is something you wouldn't wish onto your worst enemy. However, I put my hair up in combs, slathered my face with cold cream, got into a nightgown and settled onto a pillow. My eyelids had barely closed when my maid, tapping gently, opened the door a cautious crack and peered in as though she expected to see a cadaver. In a hoarse whisper she said Mister wanted me on the phone. He was sorry but it was important. I picked up the receiver and his voice, weak and quite reproachful, informed me he had just thrown up the oyster stew. I said I was awfully sorry, but was that all he had to tell me. He said well, yes, then added, "*You* try going through an opening sometime and see how you like it!" which remark, seeming to me to defy comment, I hung up.

The afternoon passed somehow. I dozed a bit and read a bit . . . an article in the *Nation* to give me a broader outlook, some pages of a book on Oriental philosophy to give me serenity. Neither did either. At five-thirty my husband came home in a state of agitation. Six years ago he lost his left leg in a coasting accident but ever since has made out admirably on a store one which never goes wrong. Today it had. Some hinge or other had cracked in the wooden foot and every step produced a deep groan. "You see?" he said accusingly. I said I did and, as in the case of the oyster stew, I was awfully sorry. He said it was all very well for me. I merely had to lie in bed and be waited on, then go on down to the theatre and act. I said again I was sorry and he said well, maybe he'd better take some bicarbonate of soda.

At six, my best friend arrived from Philadelphia. She uttered a perfunctory darling how was I and, without waiting for a reply, said I couldn't possibly know what she was going through and where did I keep the bicarbonate of soda. She appeared to be rather cross. I got out of bed, mixed her a dose and brought it to her, an attention she accepted as an obvious part of her due. After gulping down the glassful, she again told me I was incapable of knowing what she was going through; then she suddenly turned on me with a petulant, "Why you had to pick out the stage! Couldn't you have chosen a line of work that would have been easier on your friends?"

"What line of work?" I asked.

"Well," she growled, "you might become a reporter for the *National Geographic Magazine* and get sent off to distant places for long months at a time." And she banged shut her door. I retired to bed with injured dignity.

Shortly after that, my husband came into my room and informed me he had fixed the squeak in his foot with some of my typewriter oil and added, "It just goes to show." What it went to show, he didn't go on to explain. Instead, he began glaring at a picture which I had recently hung, tacking it up beside my dressing table without taking any precise measurements. "Damn it all!" he shouted in "Life with Father" tones, "Why will women do these things!" and he stormed from the room, returned with yardstick and tool kit, took down the picture, measured, moved the tack one inch to the left, rehung the picture and said, "There!" It was clear he felt better. Then he said he'd leave me to rest quietly until time to go to the theatre. Not talk to anyone. The maid would bring me my tea. I'd better have it in bed. He'd go downstairs and take care of the people he'd invited in for cocktails. I asked gently what people he'd invited in for cocktails and he hurried out saying, "Oh, just people." I gathered he hadn't the slightest idea.

My best friend, still cross, came in to ask me if I thought I was likely to trip. I said I hoped to God not. Then she asked me if I knew all my lines and I said I hoped to God so and she said she guessed she'd be all right once the curtain went up. I made the mistake of telling her that I was not in the first act.

"Not in the first ACT!" she lashed out. "Well, that's the final straw!" and once more she slammed shut her door. I didn't see her again till after the show.

My tea arrived and so did those people my husband had invited in for cocktails. One by one he dispatched them to my room, not from motives of wishing to hearten me, but because he found it too much to cope with them himself. "Run upstairs!" he halloed at each newcomer. "The old woman wants to see you! Go cheer her up." The old woman was still in a state of cold cream and combs when they began to appear. They stood about the bed in a manner that made me feel the anesthetist would come along shortly and we'd all go together to the delivery room. Their combined method of cheering me up resolved itself into variations on a single theme. Some looked gallant and said not to mind, they were going through it all with me, some shook their heads and said they wouldn't be an actress for anything on God's green earth and some beamed brightly and said, "Well, well! Tonight's the night, isn't it?"

Time which had hitherto dragged by on leaden feet now, as my hour of trial approached, began to fly at rocket speed. I rose, dressed and hurried downstairs. The group in the living room, now on their third round of cocktails, were still telling each other how nervous they were. As I paused in the doorway, they

111

called out desultory words of encouragement on the "happy landing" order, two kissed me mournfully and one actually helped me on with my coat. I rang for the elevator, the doorman got me a taxi and I went down to the theatre completely alone.

The play fortuitously got over. I neither tripped nor forgot my lines and none of my loved ones in the audience had to be carried out. After the final curtain, the usual first nighters flocked behind with the usual theatrical insincerities. My friends and family flitted in for a brief moment to tell me how relieved they were and that they'd see me back at the house. Some of them volunteered to carry a few boxes of flowers home for me, a kindly attention in the execution of which they managed to lose quite a few of the cards. I removed my warpaint, got into civilian attire and left the theatre. Nobody had stayed around to escort me home. A compassionate stage-hand hailed me a cab. I arrived at my apartment to find a party going on in full swing. My entrance was unnoticed except by a small group near the door who uttered polite cries of welcome. One gentleman approached me with a fresh highball, held it toward me and, just as I was about to grab it, drained it down himself. His companion, a lady whom I hardly knew, rushed up to me, embraced me and expostulated, *"Darling!* You were wonderful! But, then all you had to do was act. Just let me tell you a little of what I went through!"

Parcel of Land

I DIDN'T KNOW

Parcel of Land

t is enlightening to learn that one's preconceptions of seemingly everyday transactions are completely erroneous. Take, for example, the purchase of a piece of real estate. For a number of years we have lived in the country in a rented house which we recently decided to buy. Our landlord was willing to sell; the price had been settled upon and mine was the simple fantasy that all there remained to do was sign a document, hand a check over the back fence and set up at the entrance gate a smart little black sign bearing our name in gold letters. But that, it seems, is not the way one goes about it. The house is in a location a good fifty miles out on Long Island; so was the gentleman from whom I was buying it, and so, at the time, was I. Therefore, the formal purchase had to be effected in Wall Street.

It was a shock to learn that property deeds, like

divorce papers, have to be handled by lawyers. It was a continuation of the shock when my phone rang and a lady with a brisk voice informed me she was the secretary to Mr. X., my real estate lawyer (it was the first I knew I had one), and would I please be at Mr. X.'s office for the closing of the deed Wednesday morning at nine-thirty? Not being an early riser, I asked her politely if the appointment couldn't possibly be put off till a later hour; to which she replied, politely, that it couldn't possibly be. Deed signing, like operations, for some reason, have to take place early in the morning. Tuesday evening a pal from Chicago took me out on what he laughingly called the town, a term for the shortest distance between the Copacabana, El Morocco and the Stork Club; and Wednesday morning, after a savage alarm clock had brought me back to reluctant consciousness, I lay for a space wondering miserably what good any of the property could be to me now with the possible exception of that little green plot in the pine grove.

By dint of inner fortitude and black coffee, I trembled into some clothes, selecting the soberest in my wardrobe. It was raining, and the added note of rubbers and the only available umbrella to be found in the hall closet, which was a large cotton man's affair, was, I hoped, one of substantial respectability. Bravely I emerged, found my way to the nearest subway station and managed to board a downtown train. Wall Street always frightens me, and lawyers' offices frighten me even more. I wanted to say to the girl at the reception desk, "Please tell them I've come to make a clean confession." Moreover, Mr. X., my newly acquired real estate lawyer was, it seemed, a member of one of those impressive firms with a name like Threadwell, Hayes, Plunkett, Farmer and Sinus, and their outer office was only a degree less imposing than the entrance vestibule of the White House. Paneled walls formed a cream-colored background for candelabra which might have come out of Mount Vernon and only my rubbers kept me from skidding across the black marble floor.

A young lady at an Early Colonial switchboard inquired if she might do something for me. When I'm particularly overawed, I'm apt to go nervously folksey, and I heard myself babbling something to the effect of how did she do and yes indeed she *could* help me . . . I'd bought a house, that is I hadn't quite bought it because I had to be here to buy it, although it itself was fifty miles out on Long Island . . . *in* Long Island. The young woman put a merciful stop to my babbling by saying she guessed I wanted to see Mr. X. and please what was the name. After a little thought I told her and she plugged in a call to Mr. X., telling him I was there. The effect of this information to Mr. X. is food for speculation for after imparting it, she listened for several suspensive seconds, murmured a laconic, "I see, sir," unplugged the connection and, with a look which implied that she certainly knew all about *me*, asked if I'd be kind enough to wait. I said I'd be kind enough to and

pulled out one of six Sheraton chairs which were
grouped around a polished table. It made a rasping
noise and the girl turned to look. The table was strewn
with reading matter for the edification of waiting
clients . . . the morning *Tribune,* some *Time Maga-
zines,* a stray *Life* and the latest edition of *Fortune,*
a publication which impresses me very much because
I can't understand it. In 1928, I daresay *Spur* and *The
International Studio* may have swelled the list of
periodicals. Now, as a concession to the dawning new
world, a few dog-eared copies of *Cue* had found their
way into the collection. I didn't try to read, partly
because I had left my glasses at home and partly because the way I was feeling I wasn't sure I still knew
how. I just sat. Very still. Except for one unfortunate
moment when, in spite of all efforts to stifle it, I
emitted one lone loud hiccough. The young lady again
turned and I turned, hoping to see someone behind
me onto whom to fasten the guilt. The only thing
behind me was a steel engraving of Thomas Jefferson,
and the sight made me sigh over the sorry depths to
which American womanhood has sunk since the days
of the lions. I continued to wait, and for a time everything was very hushed. Then, a distant door opened
and two men advanced along the corridor conversing
in low tones on a subject which appeared to be not
only secret but of grave import to the state. One of the
gentlemen, wearing a dark overcoat and carrying a
bowler, was obviously a Titan in the world of finance
and the cares of his position showed in distinguished

furrows on his pallid face. The other man, having neither hat nor overcoat, was apparently a member of the firm and, as they drew near, I, with a start of joy recognized him as a close friend and neighbor whose sentiments for me, I had hitherto fatuously believed to be those of admiration not untinged with a certain amount of respectful prurience. Certain that he would be overjoyed to see me, I leapt to my over-shod feet and rushed over to him with outstretched hand and cheery, "Hello, Toots!" He looked at me blankly while the captain of industry turned to him with an expression which clearly read, "Do you know this woman or shall I ring for the guard?" For a moment, I thought that my friend was having his little joke but I was reckoning without the way of a lawyer in his lair. After an awkward pause, a cold light of recognition came into his eye, he gave me a stiff bow and the smile an elderly uncle manages to force over the head of a small child who has just slapped a mud pie on his white flannels, muttered a staid, "How do you do?" and continued his ambulatory conference with his distinguished client. I slunk back to my Sheraton chair and tried to read an article in *Fortune*. It was illustrated with graphs which looked to me so much like the fever chart of my own present state of debility, I gave it up.

After a time a bright-looking young man appeared and, with some hesitancy, asked if I were Mrs. So-and-So. Somewhat apologetically, I said I was. He was quite a presentable young man and I rather wanted

to explain that this was a bit early in the morning for
me and please not to think that I always looked this
way. I vaguely hoped he might be Mr. X., my real
estate lawyer, but he informed me he was a Mr.
Whitby and that he'd come to take me to Mr. X. Mr.
Whitby was, I gathered, a sort of legal intern in the
place. Trying to rise above my rubbers and umbrella,
I followed him down a hallway and up a palatial
stairway, along another corridor and on to the open
door of Mr. X.'s office. Mr. X., a distinguished-looking
gentleman, greeted me with a solemn, "How do you
do, Mrs. So-and-So, I'm Mr. X."; and, not to be out-
done in matters of legal etiquette, I answered, "How
do you do, Mr. X., I'm Mrs. So-and-So." With great
courtesy he asked me to be seated, indicating a line
of heavy chairs which were drawn up at the sort of
massive table around which one imagines peace con-
ferences are negotiated. I chose a place down at the
end, in a position that was definitely below the salt.
Mr. X.'s manner was so politely solemn, I wanted
gently to remind him that it was about buying the
house, not reading the will; but before I could, there
entered another gentleman, carrying a brief case. He
approached Mr. X. and, in a tone of deep bereave-
ment, announced that he was Mr. Beddoes, attorney
for the seller. This surprised me and quite hurt my
feelings. Why should the seller, whom I regarded as
a good friend, require an attorney? Didn't he trust
me? Maybe he did but it was obvious Mr. Beddoes
didn't. After being formally introduced, he gave me

a look of considerable doubt, gathered his brief case to his bosom and betook himself to the furthermost end of the Dumbarton Oaks table.

Another brief-cased gentleman walked in and informed Mr. X. that he was Mr. Fenner, closer for some sort of Title Corporation. I had no idea what a closer was, but, judging by Mr. Fenner's bearing, I gathered it must be mighty serious business. He bowed distantly to me and took a seat also at the far end of the table. Mr. Fenner was followed by Mr. Coogan who said he was from the office of Henry Rafferty, whatever that meant. There then arrived a Mr. Davison, who stated that he had come to acknowledge the mortgage. I hadn't fully realized there was to be a mortgage until Mr. Davison expressed his willingness to acknowledge it. The word has a sound of doom for me and I had a premonitory picture of our little family being turned out of the old homestead on the eve of the final payment.

The seller, my landlord, then appeared and it was somewhat cheering to note that the gentlemen at the far end of the table greeted him as they had me, politely but definitely as an outsider. He modestly took the chair beside me and for a time we exchanged shy snatches of conversation in the mournful manner of parishioners waiting for service to start.

A few further individuals made their appearances, some ladies who I gathered were secretaries, a little gray man whose identity remained a mystery and an unhappy-looking office boy who handed Mr. X. something that looked like an enormous diploma. It proved to be the blueprint of my property and Mr. X. opened it out on the table, asking if I would please verify it as being a correct map of my "intended parcel of land." The phrase made the whole transaction sound slightly shoddy. I don't understand maps any too well and without my glasses I couldn't even make out the white lines, but I rose and leaned over it with careful scrutiny, trying my best to look like General Eisenhower planning a campaign. Mr. X. nodded to one of the secretaries who started reading off an interesting, if completely incomprehensible, survey of the place, couched in a verbiage akin to that of boxing the compass. Instead of "left by the Jones' cornfield," which is what I would have said, she rattled off a lot of stuff about "north, so many degrees so many *seconds*" which struck me as peculiar. What struck me as not only peculiar but definitely depressing was the list of landmarks they had picked out to define my boundaries. "Southeast by three decayed trees," the young woman read, or "west around stagnant swamp," or even "due north past large manure pile." My neighbor, the seller, shifted his feet uneasily and I began to wonder if maybe my "parcel of land" might not prove to be something akin to Riker's Island.

Then began an extended period of signing things. Mr. Beddoes produced a document to which, he explained, "$44.00 in revenue stamps were to be affixed and canceled upon acceptance of the deed and payment therefor," which seemed elaborate but impressive. Mr. Fenner, after examining it with an air of respect and suspicion, passed it on to Mr. X., who announced it to be in order and handed it on to me, asking me to please read and sign it. Even if I had had my glasses it is doubtful if I would have been able to read, much less understand it. Shyly I asked just what it was. In shocked astonishment Mr. X. said, "The Deed," and I said, "Oh," and signed. As I did someone, I think it was Mr. Coogan, said, and it's all I remember him saying ever, "The deed contains no covenants except the one required by the lien law," to which I murmured that that was indeed comforting as I certainly didn't want any covenants. The Deed was followed by the Statement of Closing Figures and Adjustments which had to do with a village tax and a town tax. Wondering why there should be both, I asked if the elders of our country hamlet hadn't made up their minds yet whether we were a town or a village. I guess Mr. X. didn't know because his only reply was, "If you'd just sign here, please." He then handed me two documents which he said were affidavits in regard to my citizenship. Not without some slight indignation, I asked if there was anything wrong with my citizenship and Mr. X., with an indulgent smile, explained, "It's to induce the Title Company to issue a policy to insure your title fee and the other is to induce the Title Company to insure the mortgage." Expressing the hope that the Title Company would prove to be easily induced, I signed both papers. As I did, I heard someone say that something, I didn't

123

get just what, was "in escrow." For years I've been planning to take a day off and learn just what "escrow" means and what happens to things that are in it, who puts them in and how long they stay in it. I have a mental picture of "escrow" as being a sort of deep-freeze arrangement located in the nethermost bowels of a bank. Everybody seemed relieved that whatever it was, was now in it, and I felt relieved, too.

After all this, I was asked to make out a number of checks in payment, not for the house, but for some interesting items such as an appraisal fee, a credit report and a tax accrual.

I found myself becoming a little frantic. All in the world I had wanted was simply to buy a small piece of property. "Wouldn't it be simpler," I asked, "if I just sent out for some beads, a keg of rum and a few muskets?" The gentlemen obviously didn't think it would be and I was hastily silenced by Mr. Fenner who, in a nervous voice asked the seller if he was ready to surrender the lease. The seller said he was and surrendered it. I was disappointed that no sword went along with it. And that last bit of drama closed the meeting. Mr. X., with the smile of a person who has just tied the knot, informed me that I now owned the house and land. At what moment during all these formalities it came into my possession I shall never know. Everybody shook hands with everybody but me and I hastened out of the building and made a bee-line for the Penn Station and the first available Long Island train. I wanted to see my land. After all

124

this, I was afraid it might have grown into a second Louisiana Purchase. The local pulled in at the little rural stop, I got out and hailed Mr. Moore, our lone taxi man and, with palpitating heart, started for the place. As we turned in at the gate, I was almost afraid to look. I needn't have been. The house hadn't turned into a replica of Chenonceau and my "parcel of land" looked to me just the same. That hole in the road still needed filling in, the top hinge of the screen door had broken loose and a dog very much in need of a bath came to greet me, carrying the remains of my best and last suède glove. I heaved a sigh of recognition. "Thanks for driving me home, Mr. Moore," I said.

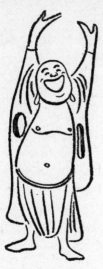

Seaweed Sewer

AND DOLLY IS ITS MADAM

Seaweed Sewer

Excerpts

(With moderate apologies to Mr. Steinbeck.)

u Hung, the Chinaman, flap-flapped to the sagging door of his sagging shop and looked out at the sunshine which flashed like sharp little diamonds on the tin cans, the broken bottles and the dream suspended in time. Seaweed Sewer was waking up . . . stretching its garbage laden arms, yawning . . . its great, warm, glorious maw open to the dawn and the sky and the particles blowing in from the municipal disposal plant. Bud and the boys who lived in the Palace Outhouse were already starting the routine of their harmoniously fuguelike daily existence. Sammy was heating coffee in a Sherwin-

Williams paint can, Herb was parting his hair with the one community fork and Lillian was thoughtfully picking lice out of the frayed seams of the striped shirt that he had saved from the penitentiary. Lillian was named that because when he was born his mother, who at the time was full of dandelion wine and Peruna, thought the baby was the spitting image of Lillian Russell and, after fourteen childbirths, she had somewhat lost her ability of distinguishing between the boys and the girls.

Across the ash dump, Minna Morrison was setting out a saucer of milk for the five good-natured brown rats. They were her pets. She loved them and gave them tea parties every afternoon. The rats sat on little doll chairs and Minna fed them rationed cheese and bits of steak and let them nibble holes in her husband's payroll. Tom Morrison didn't mind. He knew the rats meant poetry and truth to Minna. Tom is a wise man and seldom sober.

Bert Malone had come out for his morning's deep-breathing exercises on the hassock of parched earth formed by a leak in the gas main. Bert Malone and his wife, Mrs. Bert Malone, live in a deserted privy which they have fixed up with instinctive taste. There are little organdy curtains at the windows; hand-painted stove lids cover the former seat holes and a night-blooming cereus clutches with hungry tendrils at the half-moon of the doorway.

Dad was out with his butterfly net and his morning growler of ale. Dad worked for Western Pathological.

130

When the tide was right he collected the fabulous yield of the bay . . . sea anemones, iridescent limpets, lovely old barnacles, wavy steamers of eel-grass and speckled grapefruit shells. Sponges, mops, buttle-stars, urchins, orphans and waifs. He gathered them with his long slender fingers, tender as a woman's, placed them lovingly in the growler of ale, then took them back to the laboratory and gently ate them while his gramophone played Palestrina records.

Nobody was stirring yet at the Bear Grease Restaurant. The Bear Grease is not a restaurant, but Dolly who runs it has to call it that because the respectable, hypocritical, ulcer-raddled citizens of Monterey would never have countenanced its true title. It is a lovely heart-warming, humanitarian whorehouse and Dolly is its madam . . . beautiful, kind, gold-toothed, sanctified and usually ossified . . . Lillith in a housecoat, Ceres with dyed red hair, Dolly, the Earth Mother of Seaweed Sewer. She is misunderstood by the matrons of the town, horrible blind creatures, leading ugly pinched lives of keeping house and bathing, bearing children and planting gardens.

Everyone wanted to give Dad a party. Rumors flew about Seaweed Sewer like angry blowflies about Mac's garbage dump and people were busy collecting presents. Mr. Malone, who knew a thing or two about antiques, had worked for days fixing up a fine old water-closet chain and handle. Using crankcase oil he'd appropriated from a parked police car, he had polished the handle into a patina of renaissance splendor, while the chain sparkled with the glory of Dolly's diamond sunburst. Gustave, the sculptor (Gustave wasn't his name and he wasn't a sculptor), was making Dad a rope of wet sand. The beauty of that was, when the sand dried, the whole thing disintegrated. The girls at Dolly's took time out from their regular work, although there was a convention of beachcombers that week and business was booming like the surf at La Jolla, to make Dad a set of ashtrays decorated in cigar bands they received as pay from their routine customers.

At the Palace Outhouse Sammy, Lillian and the boys . . . the Graces, the Muses, the Parcæ, the Holy Inquisition . . . mulled over the problem of drinks. Bud, whose only aim in life was to make everybody happy, was all for breaking into the liquor store and borrowing a case or two. But Joe said Dad would feel more at home with the wining jug. The wining jug was a lovely, shimmering, pulsing concoction of tequila, vodka, Southern Comfort, minestrone, Seven Up and Virginia Dare. Joe no longer added Mother Sills to the mixture. It made the whole thing taste too much like pink lemonade, he said.

The party was the all high in Seaweed Sewer society functions. Everyone came. The girls from Dolly's, the Malones, Hu Hung the Chinaman, and any number of unknowns, hardy souls who only asked to fight. Things were slow getting started. People just sat around quietly and got stinking. Mac turned on the gramophone, playing a cracked record of "In My Harem" over and over while Dad read aloud a poem in Icelandic. A golden thing of carnal beauty, it reminded them all of their mothers and Dolly sobbed pleasantly into the wining jug. Then things began happening. Sammy playfully called one of the unknowns a cad and the unknown playfully knocked out Sammy's front teeth. Everything went finely from then on. People began breaking things over each other's heads, first gramophone records, then plates and finally the Mason jars containing Dad's specimens. Released from their confinement, the specimens joined in with the fun. The floor was strewn with broken glass, teeth and a few eyes. Things were just getting good when the police arrived to say that there was a complaint from the people across the street . . . gross insensitive persons who lived in houses, raised families and had the smug effrontery to earn their own livelihoods. But the police weren't a bad lot, really. One quick glance at the wreckage, the teeth, the prostrate bodies and they caught the spirit of the party. They took off their holsters and coats and decided to stay on a while. Toward five they went, police and all, and smashed the windows of the houses across the way.

Next morning, Dad rose with a throbbing head, a heaving stomach and a bad case of bronchitis. He was serenely happy. He turned on a record of Mozart, opened a quart of ale, threw up a little and started sweeping up the place. A cockroach watched him with steady, ancient eyes. The tide rose in foaming, bubbling lapets, the sun sparkled on the mosaic of jagged glass and bottle tops and the great god of the Dunghill smiled in quiet benediction.

Those Friends of His

"MOM, STRUTHER'S DYING"

Those Friends of His

t is a debatable point as to how well most parents ever really know their children. How well they ever really know their children's friends is another point and one which, at least speaking for myself, is not even debatable. For my son's acquaintances have always been shrouded in a curious mystery which I long ago gave up attempting to solve. Let me hasten to say that there is nothing wrong with any of them . . . on the contrary, they all seem to be very acceptable and often quite delightful young persons. But also they all seem to hail from a region located beyond an Iron Curtain which recognizes no parental passport. To be sure, those who come to the house are always politely introduced to my husband and me, but beyond the mere pronouncement of their names we are vouchsafed no further enlightenment.

How or when he has met them, we are never told and we have learned that to ask him questions regarding their families or habitats, is the equivalent in tactlessness of asking for their Wasserman reports. By this I do not wish to give the impression that our son is a secretive or particularly reticent type. His is an amiably outgoing nature and with his parents he is always most communicative . . . except when it comes to his friends. I am quite certain that he is in no way ashamed of his buddies and the horrid suspicion that he might perhaps be ashamed of his parents, I put rapidly away as unworthy. I guess it just strikes him as too complicated to explain us to one another.

This has been the case ever since our offspring started carving out his own social life . . . to be specific, since the day he toddled away from our bench in the park to grasp the immense hand of an immensely Irish policeman with whom he carried on a long and apparently solemn conversation, after which he toddled back to the bench and put a quietus on maternal curiosity as to the gentleman's identity with a terse "He's a friend of mine." His response to further probing concerning whence this friendship had sprung was still terser: "I just know him." Then, waxing expansive, he added, "He's Officer McKenna." At that period of tiny tothood, with the spectacular exception of Officer McKenna, his set of friends was hardly of his own choosing . . . being composed either of the children of my own acquaintances or the small charges of his various nurses' co-tyrants . . . a traditional injustice which, from time immemorial has surely been shared with mutual resentment by all small fry who, as victims of the well-bred juvenile code, have been submitted to this form of gregarious forcible feeding.

The influx of unidentifiable companions began about the time we had decided to live in the country for a couple of years and our child was ten. It had been our idea to extract him from the little-gentlemanly atmosphere of one of those expensive Manhattan day academies whose scholars wear a diminutive cap bearing a heraldic insignia, refer to their instructor as Master and address him as Sir, and to expose him to a more democratic, if less intellectually stimulating, way of life in a rural public school whose scholars wore either no caps or the sort that said "Purina Chows," referred to their instructor as Teacher and addressed her as Hey. At first, when he would make an announcement to the effect that he was bringing home someone named Jimmy or Leroy (pronounced *Lee*-roy) to supper, if I committed the maternal blunder of asking who was Jimmy or *Lee*-roy (even bravely echoing the pronunciation), I soon learned to hope for no further elucidation than a cryptic "A friend of mine." The Jimmies and *Lee*-roys were all very nice little boys. At least so they appeared to be, for my only means of estimating their characters was during the brief period of supper, a repast to which our young visitors paid tribute with lively voracity and dead silence. No time was wasted on idle chit-chat. As for drawing them out, any conversational ball-tossing on my part either landed with the resiliency of a horseshoe in sand or was returned with monosyllabic finality. Occasionally my son, in an access of Rotarian geniality, would make an opening for one of his pal's better anecdotes with some such introduction as "Hey, *Lee*-roy, tell about how your father got his hand caught in the tractor." And the *Lee*-roy of the evening, after a pause that would have done credit to Maurice Evans would, without looking up from his plate, come forth with a carefully thought out "Well, you know my Dad? Well, he got his hand caught in a tractor." My son might then add encouragement with an enthusiastic "He had to have stitches taken, didn't he?" Which expansion of the theme our guest would cut short with a hollow "Ten," and, except for a feeble "How awful" or "My!" from me, that would be that. Where the Jimmies or *Lee*-roys lived, I was seldom informed more specifically than by an impatient "Oh, Mom, if I *told* you, you wouldn't *know!*" . . . an observation whose truth I was to realize on the occasion when our son (who was quarantined at home, being great with mumps) prevailed upon me to take his two pet hamsters (a highly uninspiring form of beastie whose purpose in Nature's scheme science has surely yet to discover) over to the unknown house of one of these unknown *Lee*-roys. His ostensible reason was that he feared the hamsters might come down with mumps . . . although I believe the real reason was a thorough cooling off of his affections for the miserable little mammals. After considerable difficulty, I located the *Lee*-roy home and deposited the hamsters with the *Lee*-roy mother who received them with amazement and suspicion which last emotion was well justified, for the hamsters eventually came down not at all with mumps, but with a great many more hamsters in a Schmoolike fruition which proved acutely unpopular with the *Lee*-roy mother and again I realized the truth of my son's assertion that I wouldn't know where his pals lived when I drove about the countryside in a car teeming with hamsters, trying to find further dwellings of further buddies who might be bide-a-wee minded. What happened to the subsequent multiplicities of hamsters, I don't know. This was during the meat shortage and I never dared inquire.

At this tender age, that "friend of his" could always be counted upon as being of the masculine gender. Although I do recall our table being occasionally graced by the presence of one *femme fatale* who must have been all of fifteen and went by the iridescent name of Opal. She was placid and amiable and there must have been a bond of affectionate reciprocity between herself and the fourth grade, for she had been repeating it for quite a number of years. And that was all that we ever knew regarding Opal.

After our offspring was dispatched to boarding-school, if I had any fatuous notion that I'd begin knowing a little more about his acquaintances, I had another guess coming. During his first Christmas

141

holiday, my blithe inquiry as to his new set of pals
was parried with the inevitable "Oh, just friends of
mine." Family exposure to one of them was eventually
risked over a week end of his spring vacation when he
told us "a guy" was coming down for the night. I not
unnaturally asked, "Who?" and he laconically replied,
"Struther." When I made bold to say, "Struther who?"
he uttered a last name that left me as uninformed as
had the first and when I made even bolder to ask
where Struther came from, he narrowed it down to
"Somewhere out West." The guy named Struther
turned out to be a pallid, rather doleful little boy and
"somewhere out West" a large city in eastern Ohio.
During his sojourn with us, we didn't learn much
more about Struther and I rather think there wasn't
awfully much to learn. My only encounter with
Struther which betokened any intimacy occurred at
two A.M. when my husband and I awoke to hear is-
suing from our bathroom curious scuffling sounds
which might have been very large mice and again it
might have been marauders. It turned out to be the
pajama-clad apparitions of our son and Struther. The
former was frantically ransacking the medicine closet
while the latter was standing apathetically behind
him, looking like a ghostly character in a William
Blake vision. Upon sight of my startled face, my son
announced in a tone that was partly sepulchral, partly
delighted . . . "Mom, Struther's dying." And indeed
it looked that way, for Struther's face was the color of
green Chartreuse. I asked him where he felt the worst,

an utterance of concern which obviously struck my son as superfluous and over late for he repeated his previous announcement of Struther's rapidly approaching demise. Trying to assume the manner of a soother of a panic-stricken crowd, I managed to restrain my child from administering last rites to Struther in the form of a combination of Bromo-Seltzer, castor oil and Stoke's Expectorant and practiced my own less spectacular therapy, which was to hold Struther's forehead while he dispensed with his latest meal and, it would seem, quite a few previous ones.

During the ensuing school years many unidentifiable lads have stayed in our house and our son has gone to stay in houses where I presume that he in turn is equally unidentifiable. For I believe that this fetish of the young for keeping their friends and activities as hush-hush as the identity and movements of warships is characteristic of the teen-ager. It consoles me to think so, at any rate. During that trying period he had a way of taking my most casual inquiry of a purely social nature in the light of a trick screening question of the F.B.I. If I asked where he was going, the reply likely as not would be "Out," and "Who with?" would be answered by the inevitable "A friend of mine." This element of mystery manifested itself particularly over the telephone when unknowns would call up and in tones of an actor in a radio thriller would ask if our offspring were home. If he was not, they'd mutter, "Oh," and there would follow

143

an ominous pause. If I asked ever so politely if there
was any message, a voice that was a dead ringer for
The Shadow would say that it would call back later.
(Sometimes the voice went into an adolescent crack
and then it seemed a lot less like The Shadow.) If he
was home, he would dive for whatever telephone extension was farthest removed from the one I was on
and, coming on the wire would say, in his own radio
utterance, "O.K., Mother, you can hang up." Toward
his mid-teens, the feminine element started raising its
pretty head . . . which was about all it ever raised.
Certainly the vocal demonstration never soared higher
than a whisper. The little girls who called up sounded
as if they were speaking over a bad connection from
Cape Town, or as if they were just coming out of ether.
They were even less communicative than the boys,
and despite my efforts to sound warmly cordial even
to a potentially fatuous mother-in-law degree, it was
all too clear that they regarded me in the light of a
menacing duenna or an agent from Moscow.

He must have been about sixteen when he received
his first long distance call. It came just before dinner
and was put in from Omaha, Nebraska, and, although
I had answered the ring on the upstairs extension, I
had, with admirable self-control, hung up before the
connection came through, albeit I was consumed with
curiosity. Not, however, of a particularly prying nature. I just thought it most unusual for anyone to be
telephoning him from Omaha, Nebraska. I restrained
myself until dinner was nearly over and then, with

elaborate casualness, asked by the way who had called him long distance. Whereat he and his father rose, shook hands and the latter handed over a quarter. It seems they had had a bet as to whether my inevitable inquiry would come before or after the dessert course. I thought it quite vulgar of them.

This attitude would have grieved the maternal heart more had I not gone over in my mind my own junior-misshood and with a belated pang of remorse for my family remembered how I must have acted in a very similar fashion. I too kept my friends pretty much of a secret. Some of them, as I recall not without a slight shudder, were best kept secret . . . and a dark one at that . . . especially that girl named Clarisse who came from Kansas City and was considered "fast" because she used rouge and wore three frat pins all at the same time. I too was mysterious in regard to phone calls. In those mechanically un-blessed days, the telephone was usually kept in the most inconvenient location one could find about a house. Ours was in a coat closet at the end of a small vestibule. If any of my buddies called me up, I'd close both the doors of vestibule and closet and smother-ing myself and my voice amid a welter of raincoats, I would carry on long and muffled conversations, the gist of which was usually a date to go over to Glocker's ice cream parlor for a banana split. If I heard the sound of approaching parental footsteps, I'd mutter hastily, "I'll have to hang up now, my mother's coming."

They grow out of it. Our son is now eighteen and these advancing years have mellowed him considerably. He no longer treats the phone as if it were a secret service mechanism and now carries on fairly intelligible conversations with his friends in our presence. He is becoming actually expansive about his acquaintances and often tells us who their parents are. And just last week, he told me in detail where he was going for the evening. Not only that, but he gave me the approximate hour of when to expect him home. Things are looking up.

French Code

A FRENCHMAN GAVE MY FANNY A PASSING PAT

French Code

he French are not a nation to embrace with enthusiasm any modernized forms of communication. They prefer the personally delivered note to the telegram and they regard that pneumatic compressed air system which, like a department-store change blower, whooshes a "petit bleu" to any given address in Paris, as far more reliable than the telephone. In this latter surmise they are undoubtedly correct. Hand a concierge an ordinary letter to mail and he stamps it with alacrity . . . which means he stamps it the moment he has finished reading the name and habitat of the prospective recipient and, in the case of a postcard, the context of the written message. Hand the same concierge a letter and ask him to send it air mail, and he attacks the job with the reluctance of an overworked notary obliged to affix unfamiliar seals to a foreign document. There follows an involved process which entails first the prolonged consulting of a book concealed below the cash drawer, then weighing the envelope both on his open palm and on a small machine which one could fancy to be the legacy of an ancestral alchemist, then producing, also from below the cash drawer, a sort of thin memory book in which he keeps his stamps. After poring over the collection with the absorption, albeit with none of the dedication, of a philatelist, he settles on one, tears it out, licks and attaches it and mournfully slips the letter into a postal almsbox, his discouraged manner indicating that he has no hopes of it ever reaching its destination. Hand the same concierge a telegram to send, and the prospect plunges him into even gloomier misgivings. Tell him it's a cable and you might as well be asking him to deliver it by rowboat.

One recent morning in the French capital, I had occasion to send a wireless to a ship at sea. My husband told me to entrust the dispatching of it to the concierge of our small hotel . . . an onerous request which I felt would completely unnerve the already overworked little man. I would, I said, attend to it myself. My husband, who, like all righteous American men, gets panic-stricken if left alone in Paris, warned me that I didn't know how to go about it and, if I did, it would take too long . . . to which I countered nonsense, I was an old Parisian hand at such things and I had at least two hours before meeting him for luncheon at that restaurant whose name he had learned to make taxi drivers understand. I hastened out to the Place de la Madeleine, joined the milling maelstrom at Cook's and, with the confidence of a small girl slipping her tiny hand into the huge paw of the corner policeman, thrust my wireless before the face of a likely looking personage behind a likely looking counter. He glanced at me in surprise then, summoning the weary, routine smile whereby employees of travel agencies attempt to soothe the demented American, informed me that telegraphic communications were not handled by Thomas Cook or any of his sons. I would have to go to a post office, although, he added, if I cared to, I might address myself to the establishment Mackay Radio which found itself just a few steps down the Boulevard des Capucines. This seemed a simple solution. It was a bright day, conducive to cheerful thoughts and it was pleasant to speculate whether the boulevard down which one sprinted was that of the monks or of the nasturtiums.

The Etablissement Mackeee-Rady-you is a place of elegance and chromium, to reach which one climbs an impressive staircase and pushes a series of heavy glass doors the first few of which are not the right one. Inside was a huge mural representing a sort of roadmap of the Atlantic and Pacific Oceans, and a long marble counter behind which was standing a suave diplomatlike gentleman. To him I cheerfully presented the filled out blank. He studied the contents for a while, then raised an eyebrow, shrugged a shoulder pad and said that but this was a wireless, to which I agreed but yes. But, he said, the establissement Mack-eee handled radiograms, to which I spluttered the French equivalent of "so what." With exquisite indulgence, he went on to explain that their radio messages were sent direct to New York. I wanted to inquire why, if a radio message could get that far, it could not be intercepted at midcrossing by a ship at sea, but felt it was hardly the time for a discussion on the nature of telegraphy. Like the man at Cook's, he too said I must address myself to a post office. Then, softening somewhat, he admitted that occasionally they handled such exigencies for their special clients. I assured him that while I might not be special, I was at least a client and that I should be most reconnaissant if he would be so amiable as to charge himself with my communication in this instance. He said that well voluntarily would be do so but . . . and his hands executed that Gaelic gesture which dismisses responsibility as two juggler's balls to be tossed to the winds . . . it was his superior who must first pass on such deviation of rules. His superior had stepped out for a little instant. Perhaps Madame would have the bounty to seat herself and wait. Knowing that those little instants can extend themselves into half-hour stretches, Madame, deciding to store up her bounty, thanked the gentleman and departed in search of a post office.

I have no talent for locating post offices. Even on native soil, the only one I can find with ease is the branch in Bloomingdale's basement. I was hesitant about asking a gendarme. Morning traffic was at its frenzied height and, in dashing efforts to control it, the guardians of the law were busy waving at it those white batons resembling not so much billies as academic diplomas. Moreover, asking of a gendarme any query involves on his part a ritual to perform which he is obliged to shift his cape, tuck away the diploma, get out a black notebook and in it look up the answer, whether it be the way to the nearest Metro station, the closing hour of the Louvre or if he thinks it's likely to rain. I took the chance of setting forth in a random direction and, fortuitously came upon the familiar dark green edifice with the *Bureau de Postes,* etc. sign. I entered and found a *guichet* marked "stamps, telegraph and strangers" before which I queued up in a line of individuals each of whom was taking a very long time over his or her transaction. Eventually I found myself up at the wicket and face to face with a lady wearing a black mother hubbard and an amiable expression. At sight of the telegraphic form, her expression changed from one of amiability to one of Cassandralike foreboding, the billowy portion of the mother hubbard heaved under a deep sigh and with poised pen she approached her task as though it were one of deciphering an enemy code. After a time she looked up and said but *evidament,* this was destined for a ship in full sea, was it not. To which I agreed but yes. Oh, then, she said, one would be obliged to telephone to a bureau central because, see you, here they

153

did not occupy themselves with this here type of communication telegraphic. If I would wish to wait, she would give a blow of telephone to the bureau central because they alone knew the rates, which, she added balefully, were well high. It was clear she considered me an irresponsibly extravagant character. I assured her that while I regretted having to derange her, I should be most grateful if she *would* call the bureau central. At that, with a martyr's resignation, she stepped over to a cluttered desk, picked up the receiver of an apparatus that might have come out of F. A. O. Schwarz, rattled off an abracadabra of letters and numbers, jiggled the crossbar, then almost immediately hung up and returned to the window with the information that the bureau central was occupied . . . a state of affairs which, as far as she was concerned, appeared to close the whole foolish affair. She seemed quite relieved and her expression of amiability had returned, but it changed again to one of bale when I asked, ever so meekly, if it would be possible to try the number again in a few minutes. Well, yes, she sighed, but I knew how it was. I said that but yes I did (although it turned out that what I knew wasn't even the half of it) and how long thought she must I wait? Ah, well, she prophesied, one could not tell . . . it might be instantly, it might be a fifteen of minutes, it might be . . . and she trailed off before adding *never*. I would make better, she said, to go direct to a bureau central, a suggestion with which I concurred and asked if she knew where the nearest bureau central found itself. She turned to her fellow worker in charge of the adjacent *guichet,* a mournful man clad, like her, in a black mother hubbard; he in turn consulted another and after a bit of deliberation, the general opinion seemed to favor the Place de la Bourse. Thither I set out with renewed hope. It was still a sparkling day. Paris was still never lovelier and my spirits were still high. Moreover, a Frenchman gave my fanny a passing pat and that too was encouraging. The Bureau of Posts, Telegraphs and Telephones of the Place of the Purse is located in a subterranean corner of that edifice of high finance. Its entrance is inconspicuous to the point of near invisibility. Finding it involved circling the building twice, after asking of its whereabouts from a local news vendor whose only elucidation was a guttural *"là-bas"* and a gesture which might have indicated anything from a post office to the Tropic of Capricorn. Finally, I risked going through a sort of janitor's door and emerged into a dingy room the first whiff of which assured me I was right. Post offices the world over have an international bond, like music, in common . . . they all smell the same way, and, unlike music, it's not a nice way at all.

Again I found a wicket indicating telegrams and again confronted a mother-hubbard-clad employee, this time an irritable looking little man wearing ribboned pince-nez like Rudyard Kipling's, and once more I handed over my filled out telegraph form which by now was getting as soiled and battered as a five-franc paper bill. Again the employee, after a period of study, looked up to inform me that this was for a ship in full sea and again I replied but yes. With a sharp, pitying sigh, he handed back the form and told me in a thick Breton accent that such things must be written in ink, in block letters and "bien lisible." Discouraged but not yet despairing, I went back across the room and pulled a fresh form from a wall box above a writing counter. Having come without pen, I had to resort to the gummy wooden one supplied for public use . . . and the public had used it plenty for the nib was splayed as a canapé fork. I printed my message in block letters as *lisibly* as possible and returned to the *guichet* before which there was now quite a line-up so I, not unnaturally, went to the adjoining one, which also indicated telegrams and before which there was no line-up. The employee behind this wicket regarded me with shocked amazement. Was I not, he said, *la dame* who a moment since had addressed herself to his comerade at the next *guichet*? I confessed to being that very dame but pointed out the fact that now there was a queue at the other location. Still shocked over my breach of etiquette, he said that nonetheless I must return to his comerade who had first occupied himself of me. By the time I did so, his comerade was occupying himself of a line-up which had increased by three persons. Inching my way along, I finally arrived once more before the first comerade who accepted the proffered wire and heaved that inevitable sigh which I was beginning to suspect as being one of the French postal regulations. He pored over the contents for a time then, with an additional sigh, went over to a table and brought back a tome which contained the names, registries and telegraphic ciphers of the ships of the world. Starting with the first page of the A's, he methodically scanned each alphabetically ensuing listing with the critical absorption of a proof-reader. It was at least encouraging to realize that the entry he was searching was that of the *America* and not something like the *S.S. Zam-Zam*. The encouragement, however, was of short duration, for the little man suddenly shook his head, clucked a hopeless "Ooh la-la!" and, tossing my communication back at me, said it would be quite impossible to send it. In response to my despairing "For God's sake WHY?" he held forth the book and with a gloomily triumphant "*Voilà pourquoi*" indicated a page which listed some eight ships, all of them named *America*. How was one to tell, he said, which was the correct *America*? Obviously one could not send a telegraph wireless to all eight. But, I protested, this was for THE *America*, the important *paquebot* of the States United, the one which brought hundreds of tourists every month to France. Such Chamber of Commerce enthusiasm made no impression whatsoever on the stolid little Breton who merely repeated the fact that one could not tell and pointed again to the eight listed *Americas*. All of them, with the exception of one, were registered under Spanish or Portuguese names with home ports in the Caribbean or the Southern Hemisphere. The exception was registered in the name of the U.S. Maritime Commission and had after it a lot of abbreviations and numerals which if incomprehensible were highly impressive and I said that obviously this was THE *America*. But hold, and he impassively pointed out the entry of a similarly named craft sailing under the aegis of one Hernando Gonzales of Havana, this too was an *America*, was it not so? Perhaps . . . my voice was becoming shrill . . . but it could never be the right one . . . what would a beautiful, famous steamer-de-luxe be doing with an idiotic Cuban registry? To which he repeated his statement that one could not tell and that without the proper wireless indications a Cuban *America* or an American *America* or a God-knows-what *America* could receive a message as readily as a New York *America*. But, I insisted, if one sent it with the wireless indications of the U.S. Maritime Commission, it would not go to any other vessel and, furthermore, I was certain enough to take a chance on it being the right one. But ah, no, Madame, he said, such a hazard he could not, in all fairness to myself and the French postal system, permit. I must first obtain the correct wireless *chiffres,* to do which he advised me to go to the Compagnie of the Lines of the States United and make inquiries. But, I wailed and by now almost in tears, I had not the time . . . as it was I had already spent half the morning over this matter. It was clear he considered spending only half a morning over such transactions was getting off easy but, possibly prompted by the popular opinion that the spendthrift American will stop at no expense, he suggested that if I did not wish to go to the Line of the States United, a cabinet of telephone found itself at the end of the room, I could always use the "*appareil automatique.*" This was a rashly untrue statement on his part. I could not always use an automatic French telephone for the simple reason that I have never yet been able to use that hideous device which is certainly the apotheosis of what Alexander Graham Bell could never have had in mind. Working one, or rather trying to work one, necessitates first purchasing from a reluctant attendant a horrid little lead token which looks like something fallen out of an old hem. This one inserts into a slot on the side of the telephone apparatus, unhooks the mouthpiece and dials the number . . . all at the same time; that is, if you're lucky enough to have three hands. Then, at a given moment (which may be given but is almost immediately withdrawn), you must reach around to the other side and shove in a steel plunger . . . the sort they have on chewing-gum machines, and, if you're smart, you get your party. Not being smart, I have never gotten anything . . . neither my party nor a stick of chewing-gum nor even my lead token returned to me. This occasion proved no exception. Moreover, it had the additional complication of my first having to look up the number of the United States Lines, and this was even further complicated by the fact that the local copy of the

Paris telephone book was not to be found and the
number had to be sought in one of those voluminous
directories known as the Bottin, in which one looks
up the desired subscriber's number under such ir-
relevant headings as Professions, Departments and
Streets. Why I bothered to look it up, I can't imagine,
for having found and dialed it, I, of course, never
reached it. However, I pretended I had and when,
after the usual wait in line, I again returned to my
Breton employee I informed him with a liar's assurance that the Maritime Commission listing was the
correct one. He acquiesced, rather to my amazement,
for I half feared he might demand a written statement from the company, and agreed to send the message. I was naïve enough to imagine I could now
perpetrate a hasty getaway, but I was reckoning without having first to wait for him to figure out costs . . .
a process which meant assessing the amount per
word, plus a tax, plus an involved percentage which
might have been for service charges, the State, or a
fund for the preservation of black mother hubbards.
All this was computed through a form of higher
mathematics which at times looked like a reckoning
of light years from the planet Pluto. It was a complicated process and one in which he himself could not
have had much faith for he did the whole thing over
twice then verified it by plain everyday arithmetic
and finally went over it all step by step with his
comerade of the adjacent *guichet,* as though it were
a move in a chess tournament. It was now exactly two

hours and fifteen minutes since I had left the hotel. I was late for lunch and I knew that my husband waiting at the restaurant would be doing so in that terrible attitude of patience which every wife knows is the essence of anything else but. He was. However, he managed to ask . . . somewhat icily . . . if I had sent the wireless. I panted that yes indeed I had. "What did it say?" he asked. "Oh," I replied, "just WELCOME TO PARIS. Did you order us a cocktail, darling?"

Backstage
Performance

LOVABLE OIL MAN FROM TEXAS

Backstage Performance

'm willing to believe that it takes all sorts of people to make a world, and I suspect that most of them, at one time or another, come around backstage and visit an actress in her dressing room. If you are the actress, you're glad when they turn up, because if they didn't, you'd feel certain you were slipping. On the other hand, you sometimes wonder what under heaven prompted them to come backstage in the first place, and you get the impression that they're wondering precisely the same thing.

There is one type—people you've met once or twice —that turns up quite unsummoned and unheralded, and stays on and on. And not once during the protracted visit do these people so much as mention the performance. You don't, of course, expect all dressing-room callers to go overboard about the show, or even to have liked it; you merely expect them to mention it. But these people are the sort that hardly mentions anything. They greet you with a *"Hello,* there!," which is followed by an animated "Well!," and then they lapse into silence and an expectant expression that politely indicates that it's up to you to carry on from there. Carrying on from there resolves itself into the formula "Have you seen the Smiths lately?" "No, we haven't seen the Smiths lately, have you?" "No, I haven't seen them at all." "Neither have we. We haven't seen them at all." This peters out into another expectant "Well!," which you feel must surely be followed by a belated "We adored your show" or, if that is an over-optimistic hope, at least a polite "We thought your costumes were awfully pretty." But the nearest they get to the subject is possibly an inquiry as to what you think your next play is going to be. So, after another "Well!," back you go to cudgelling your memory for the names of mutual acquaintances other than the Smiths, whom neither of you have seen at all lately.

Another class of callers who get into a dressing room and then don't know how to get out are students —the kind who arrive in a large group shepherded by a teacher of that mysterious and frightening subject known as "voice." The teacher is usually a brisk little woman who informs you she's the Drama Department at Ingledale and she's brought her young voice people to say hello. The young voice girls mass up in a sort of Don Cossack formation that half leads you to think they are about to sing. They don't sing. They merely stand quite still and stare at you with that absorbed, unwavering expression people assume when suddenly confronted with an actress. They don't even utter that hello their teacher has promised. They just wait for you to break the ice—a tough assignment, because you haven't even the Smiths in common to talk about not having seen anything of lately. Conversation is purely a one-sided affair in which you flounder along with a few sprightly comments about my goodness, gracious me, what a lot of them there are, and are they all studying (and you brace yourself) voice? If they are, there's no way of proving it, for their only reaction is a continuation of the unwavering stare. Sometimes the teacher comes to the rescue with a few words of her own, but as they consist, as often as not, of asking you if you won't give them a message to take back to the rest of the Ingledale girls, the rescue isn't spectacular.

Then, there is the woman who just simply had to see you because she's supposed to look like you. Her friends, it appears, are always saying that she's your absolute double. It is obviously an odd thing for her friends to be always saying, but as the lady places her face up alongside yours in a pose like a 1915 camera shot of the Dolly Sisters and says "See?," you leer bravely into the mirror and croak out how extraordinary and that yes, indeed, you are flattered.

Occasionally, you are visited by one of those hearty females who once went to school with you. Her hearti-

ness has grown a trifle wheezy, and the idea of her
ever having been a girl seems preposterous. She
steams in, her husband in reluctant tow. The husband
is usually an eminently dignified individual, with a
bearing so pontifical that you're shocked when his
effervescent spouse introduces him as Ed. With them
are two or three other couples—business associates of
Ed's and their wives, who seem to regard this backstage jaunt as being on a par with a personally conducted tour through Chinatown. Once the jolly
introductions are over, the matronly classmate starts
recalling peculiarly unfortunate phases of my school
days. She brings up the episode of my washing my
hair with a henna rinse that turned it green, laughs
indulgently over my girlhood passion hopelessly divided between a Haverford sophomore and Francis
X. Bushman, and then very likely lets fly with some
variant of "Isn't life unpredictable! I was always
summa cum laude and you were always on the proba-
tion list, and here you are on the stage and I'm just a
homebody with a husband and five children." Good
breeding prevents her from adding, "And an income
of fifty thousand a year," but you can read it between
the lines of her face. Along with all the unpalatable
reminiscences, the matter of age inevitably raises its
grisly head. "I was telling them at dinner at the Union
League," she burbles happily, "I was saying 'Why,
Cornelia's just exactly the same age as I am! Would
you believe it?' " To which "Hell, no!" seems hardly
the gracious answer.

168

She and her like constitute only a small percentage of the great category of the age-conscious. A week never passes without the visit of a date-obsessionist, who starts in with "I hate to admit how many years ago I first saw you." Hating it as she does, it's surprising with what alacrity she continues with the guilty admission that it was back in 1932, in Des Moines, that a group of them came in from Junior High, and, oh, was it snowing that night, and she knows it was 1932, because that was just the year before she got married and her husband—he wasn't her husband then, of course, ha-ha—was one of the party in the bus that night.

Also in the age-conscious category are those elderly theatre devotees who speak affectionately of themselves as "we oldsters" and who clearly regard you as a well-preserved contemporary. ("Well-preserved" is my own modification.) They proffer you the good-natured assurance that they, too, date back to the days when actors were actors, and you half expect them to ask if you were on the stage of Ford's Theatre the night Lincoln was shot. A lady from this group recently swooped in after a matinée, just when I was trying to be seductive as all getout to a Yale reporter, and burst forth breathlessly with "My dear, I know you can tell me—what *has* become of Nance O'Neill and *what* is Maude Adams doing?" And then there was the whimsical little crone who turned up after an opening night in Los Angeles. Her visit coincided with that of an actor-producer who had come back with a

169

director, a starlet, and an awesomely powerful agent; she elbowed her way past these dazzling and potentially helpful luminaries, thrust at me a fistful of yellow and white begonias, and carolled in tones for all the picture industry to hear, "Greetings! Greetings from your Bryn Mawr friends of 1902."

An inevitable caller, when you're on the road, is the local amateur prima donna, whose true vocation was, of course, the professional theatre—only just as she was embarking for Broadway armed with a letter from someone who knew someone who knew Brock Pemberton, she got sidetracked into matrimony. She is apt to start the conversational ball rolling with "*Dah*-ling! *Every*one talks to you about your performance, so I'm simply not going to." So, instead, she talks about her own in the forthcoming production of "The Philadelphia Story" by the Greasepaint Club. Her manner is one of casual charm—a happy mixture of the Group Theatre and the Du Barry Success School, with just a dash of Mrs. Leslie Carter—and her language glitters splendidly with words like "tempo," "timing," and "dynamics." She refers to their forthcoming production as "The Story" and calls your line of work "the commercial theatre." Often as not, she informs you that she's been so busy with rehearsals—you, too, know how it is—she hasn't got around to seeing *your* show.

One honey of a backstage visitor is that big, overgrown, lovable oilman from Texas who was the life of a clambake on Cape Cod two summers ago. He blows in, as big and overgrown as ever but a lot less lovable and a great deal more intoxicated, accompanied by two lifelong friends he has acquired during the course of a busy afternoon. Timing his arrival with the rise of the second-act curtain, he halloos out the tidings that he isn't seeing the show but, doggone, he just happened to notice your name on the poster outside there and he had to drop in to give you a great, big surprise, because you sure were sweet to him that time at that old clambake, and he wants you to meet these two wonderful young friends of his—this wonderful little lady, who is a buyer for an exclusive store in Toledo, and this wonderful smart fellow here, who if ever you get a ticket in Bergen County let him know because he practically owns the po-lice. The wonderful little lady can just about navigate, and the wonderful smart fellow just about can't. The big, lovable Texan suggests in such a big, lovable voice that you join up with them for a nightcap after the show that the stage manager intervenes with the announcement that the curtain is up and all visitors will please leave.

Every now and then, the backstage visit takes on a disturbing, even menacing aspect. I am thinking specifically of a time in Boston when two hollow-eyed, gaunt women—a mother and daughter, I decided—stalked into my dressing room unannounced, settled down in chairs as if to spend the evening, fixed me with a look that indicated they knew where the body was buried, and uttered a sepulchral "Hello." I bleated back an astonished "Hello" and waited. After a suspenseful pause, the mother said, still in "Inner Sanctum" tones, that they hadn't seen me since Butte. And the daughter echoed no, not since Butte.

I laughed indulgently. "You must be thinking of someone else," I said, "because—funny thing, ha-ha—I've never played in Butte."

"No," said the mother, "it was Butte," and the daughter echoed, "Yes, Butte."

"But I've never even played in the State of Montana," I said.

"No," the mother continued in the same even tone, "but you used to live there." I assured her, in a voice that was growing momentarily more shrill, that I had never lived there. "When you were a girl," the mother said, and the daughter added, "Back in those days." For a few more ghastly minutes, we continued to debate the matter. The mother's cool, sinister confidence was beginning to undermine my own. It occurred to me that as a child I had once had typhoid fever and that maybe it had affected my memory at the time and was affecting it now—maybe I had lived in Butte.

Suddenly, in the midst of my panic, I heard the mother say that their house had been right across the street from my dad's place. This jolted me into a flare-up of outraged family pride. "My father," I said with crushing dignity, "was Otis Skinner."

"I know," said the mother, and the daughter echoed a lugubrious "Uh-huh." Then, as I was racking my brains to think of an appropriate rejoinder, the mother went on, in the same level tone, "And he ran the dry-cleaning establishment across from us."

My amazement at this announcement was so intense that I was able to utter only the feeblest sort of protest. Both women rose, gave me a reproachful glare, showing that they considered I was putting on airs by thus denying my simple, homespun origins, and stalked out. After the door had closed behind them, I asked my maid in a weak voice if she had ever heard of me and my family residing in Butte. She replied no, Ma'am, she hadn't, but in a wavering manner. Apparently the strange pair had mesmerized her, too. With shaking hands, I removed my makeup and fled from the theatre to my hotel room, where I astonished a number of friends by calling them up long distance and, in the course of a random conversation, casually asking if they had ever heard of the Butte period in my life. They all said no—but I'm still not quite sure.

Kinsey Reported

"THOSE THINGS" WERE TOO SACRED TO MENTION

Kinsey Reported

ord is out that the Kinsey report on the ladies is almost ready for the press. Doubtless a good percentage of the American male population whose behavior was so graphically brought to light two years ago is anticipating the low-down on the behavior . . . or misbehavior . . . of the American female with mixed emotions of dread and glee. And doubtless also the cartoonists and professional humorists are revamping and changing the gender of their old material to have it on hand by the date of publication. It now appears that the Doctor's researches are not to be confined to the overall behavior of the American male, the American female and the mudwasp (whose nationality a divided world has yet to determine). He is making a special study of that happy and unhappy breed, the people whose professions lie in the arts. Just how their patterns differ from those of the male, the female and the mudwasp, we have yet to learn. I heard of this one day when I was lunching with a lawyer friend of Dr. Kinsey's. What prompted the gentleman suddenly to come out with "How'd you like to be interviewed by Kinsey?" I don't know. Taking time out for the mouthful I was in the process of swallowing to extricate itself from my larynx and continue on its way, I croaked an incredulous "I beg your pardon?" My lawyer friend repeated his suggestion. For some reason, which may have been the presence of a dry Martini ahead of the descending mouthful, the prospect struck me as fascinating. My reply was a simple "I can't wait."

When the first enthusiasm and the second Martini had worn off, I realized that I *could* wait after all. In fact, quite indefinitely. But this was a few hours later, and by then I feared the die was cast as the lawyer's parting words had been to the effect that he would immediately inform the Doctor of my willingness to be interviewed. Oh, well, I figured, nothing might ever come of it and besides I could always get out of an awkward situation by saying I'd received a sudden summons from Hollywood . . . a fortuitous emergency which has yet to happen to me. I finished my shopping and thought no more about the matter until I reached home and was greeted by my son with the information that someone had been playing a joke on me.

"What sort of joke?" I asked.

"Oh, some dopey friend of yours called up," he answered, "and said to tell you Dr. Kinsey had called."

"And what did you say?" I asked.

"I just said, 'Oh, yeah?' and hung up. I figured it must have been John Mason Brown."

There was a certain foundation for such a surmise. I am compelled to admit that for years this distinguished gentleman of letters and I have indulged in the childish whimsey, whenever we telephone one another, of speaking in disguised voices and announcing ourselves as Rossellini and Mrs. Roosevelt, or Mae West and Cardinal Spellman. On this occasion, however, I despaired of any hope of the call having been from Mr. Brown.

"I'm afraid, my lad," I said, "that it really *was* Dr. Kinsey."

"What would he be calling *you* about?" he asked.

"Oh," I replied in an offhand manner, "I guess he wants to interview me."

My son's eyes bugged out with incredulous astonishment. "Why would he want to interview *you*, for heaven's sake?" and without waiting for an answer he catapulted into the library to tell his father, whose comment was identical except that he didn't say *heaven*. It was clear that in their opinion I could bring

179

as little enlightening material to a Kinsey report as a child of ten could bring to the stockholder's report of General Motors. As a matter of fact, neither one appeared to believe that a prospect so fantastic could ever eventuate . . . so much so that I began to disbelieve it myself. Bright and early the following day, however, as I was downing morning coffee the phone rang and I pounced to answer it before any of my family could pick up a downstairs extension. A pleasant masculine voice asked if I was me and I said that yes this was She . . . an elegance of speech which always sounds as though one were identifying oneself with Rider Haggard's heroine. The voice went on quite easily to announce that it was Dr. Kinsey and at that, I am distressed to say, I heard myself emit a curious whoop of realization followed by a gigglingly shrill "Oh, Dr. *Kinsey!*" The doctor who by now must be astonished by nothing seemed to take my vocal flutterings as a matter of course and in a completely businesslike manner went on to say that our mutual lawyer friend had told him I was willing to give him an interview and that he was delighted to hear it. I burbled a little lamely that I was delighted to hear it, too. He explained that his time in New York was limited and could we make it Friday, which was just two days off. My immediate impulse was to duck out of it all by saying that I couldn't be sorrier but that Friday I had to go out of town. Then something in me murmured that this was no time for American womanhood to show weakness and in a feeble voice I said that Friday would be just fine. He then said that, as the interview usually took two hours, what would I say to starting it at nine in the morning. What I said was a fervent "God, no!" to myself and to Dr. Kinsey a shamed-faced admission that nine was a little early for me. Then how about ten, he inquired. I was loath to tell him that 10:00 A. M. is for me about as bad as nine for fear he'd consider this an indication of my general decadence. So I said, with forced heartiness, that ten would be just fine, after which he suggested that it might be better if the interview were held at his place rather than at mine. Not knowing anything about his place, I gave a quick thought to mine. I live in a 1908 apartment building where visitors are still announced in the entrance lobby over a battery phone system so antiquated, the doorman has to resort to the tones of a hog caller to get across any communication and the prospect of the entire block being informed that Dr. Kinsey was calling on me was somewhat unsettling. Moreover, our family retainer is an elderly virginal soul who thinks nothing of interrupting any social gathering, whether large or tête-à-tête, with current bulletins of domestic exigencies and a further disturbing prospect was the possibility of her barging into the room with the news that the exterminator had come about the pantry cockroaches at a moment when Dr. Kinsey might be putting forth some particularly cozy question, on hearing which there was the risk of her either giving notice or fainting dead away. I eagerly agreed that the meeting had best be held at

181

his place. This I pictured to be some scholarly chromium quarters, impressive with bookshelves of heavy tomes, steel filing cabinets and mysterious oddments of laboratory equipment. I imagined its locale would be in either a medical building or the science department of one of the city colleges. It came as a shock, therefore, to hear him say he'd expect me at ten sharp in his room at the Pennsylvania Hotel. Again I was strongly assailed by the impulse to duck. But again some inner discipline admonished me that I had made my bed and I must lie on it. I could only hope that by 10:00 A. M. somebody would have made Dr. Kinsey's bed and wondered, a little apprehensively, if, in the manner of the patient on the analyst's couch, I'd have to lie on *it*. Taking a deep breath, I said that this too would be just fine, as casually as though it were an everyday occurrence for me to pay morning visits to gentlemen in their rooms at the Pennsylvania Hotel. I am quite aware that this hostelry has recently changed its name to Statler but to me it will always be the Pennsylvania, just as the Avenue of the Americas will always be plain old Sixth. The idea of a bedroom in a milling convention center as a setting for a Kinsey interview, for some reason struck me as so wildly incongruous, I hung up before giving vent to another loud whoop of nervous laughter.

During the ensuing forty-eight hours I was in a divided state of mind, wondering if the forthcoming commitment were something to be kept a dead secret or entrusted to a few close friends . . . like a delicate operation or an illicit love affair. As may be surmised, I started out confiding in one or two boon companions and ended up telling almost everyone I encountered. What chiefly encouraged this wholesale dissemination of news was a study of the different ways in which people received it. Had I calmly announced that on Friday I was going to jail, or receive the Nobel Prize, or elope with the Aga Khan, their reactions could not have been more varied or more intense. Some said "WHAT?"; others were speechless, while several hammed a double take before coming out with a stunned "I beg your pardon?" It was enlightening then to wait for their next comments. Women, according to whether their type was the ultra-refined or the lustily earthy, either snorted a horrified "You *wouldn't!*" or eagerly asked if he'd interview them, too. Men reacted in kind. The Pillars of the Community, with the shocked compassion they'd have for Magdalen, asked why a nice woman would want to do a thing like that, while the heartier fellows burst out laughing, slapped my knee and said oh, boy, they'd sure like to be a fly on Kinsey's pencil. A few of those professional happy-happy-marriage ladies went into frightened postures of modesty as though they'd just been walked in on in their slips, and stated with misty-eyed piety that in their opinion "those things" were too sacred to mention, especially to anyone who'd put them into a report. I wish now I had kept track of how many times the term "those things" was employed. My secretary, a glorious gal with a heart

as big as Ireland when it comes to the welfare of
our family, looked panic-stricken and gasped, "Jesus,
Mary and Joseph! You're not going to tell him all
those things, are you?" and when I asked her all what
things, she stammered, "Well, I mean *every*thing." I
silenced her a bit brutally by asking how she knew I
had *any*thing to tell him. She left the office early that
afternoon. I think it was in order to beg Father Mur-
phy to say a special prayer for me.

If the varied adult reactions were surprising, the
youthful ones were downright discouraging. It was
all too clear that in the estimation of members of the
younger generation, Dr. Kinsey must be extending his
studies into the realms of senile behavior. My son kept
reiterating his annoying "Why would he want to interview *you!*" while my best friend's twenty-year old
daughter, with a shrill of amusement, squealed,
"What??? Miss Prim???" I felt fairly offended by their
attitude until I recalled my own juvenile one in regard to my elders. To me it was quite unthinkable that
the contemporaries of my mother, who was then in her
late thirties, could have had any remote interest in
matters of the flesh except as a horrible warning to
the young. I recall my shock when our neighbor, a
forty-three-year-old widow married a doctor who was
verging on fifty and saying to my mother, "You don't
mean to tell me that they could possibly *still!!!*" and
Mother, replying quite crossly, "I don't know what
you think you're talking about, Cornelia, but I assure
you that they can." And for the next few days I

184

scanned the obituary pages for news of the joint demise through heart attack of the doctor 'and his bride.

Friday morning my alarm went off with its customary shattering effect and I lay for a time in a state of sleepy malaise, trying to remember what train I must be due to catch and to where. Then it dawned upon me that this was the day I was taking the Kinsey plunge and I was seized with the same sort of panic I felt the morning of my wedding when I scribbled a note saying, "Dearest, I shall always love you but I can't make it up the aisle," and would certainly have bolted by the next bus if there had been one. I quieted myself with the realization that after all the situations were hardly parallel and I was not about to pledge myself to journey down life's highway hand-in-hand with Dr. Kinsey. Nervously pooh-poohing such girlish fantasies, I rose with splendid energy. What to wear was a bit of a problem. The day was bleak and raw with a gusty wind and a drizzle of rain, weather which called for practical clothes. A tailored suit would have been the obvious choice. I seldom wear my one tailored suit because I think it makes me look rather like a Dean of a State Teacher's college. Fearing that this might set Dr. Kinsey off on the wrong track, I selected instead a simple street dress and pinned it at the neck with my great-grandmother's brooch by way of a talisman. Fastening the catch, I wondered if within the next two hours there'd occur a slight upheaval over the quiet Massachusetts grave where the respectable old soul lies.

I was thankful to be able to slip out of the house without any disheartening comments from my family who seemed to have forgotten about my early morning appointment. I hailed a taxi and with debonair nonchalance announced my destination. The driver proved to be the chatty type. He told me he was about to have a session with a doctor and, just to be folksy I told him I was about to have a session with a doctor, too. He said his was throat and I said well, mine wasn't throat exactly and we let it go at that.

The anticipated convention was swarming the lobby of the Pennsylvania. My qualms returned as I made my way through the crowd and up to the information desk which was so jammed I had to stand waiting in line. When my turn came, it required all my courage to ask for the number of Dr. Kinsey's room. Due to the surrounding hubbub, the clerk failed to catch the name and I was forced twice to repeat it, in an increasingly amplified voice. The clerk, with an enlightened "Oh, yes," told me the number while the rest of the line-up stared at me in fascination. Blushing prettily, I thanked him and walked over to the house phone.

The doctor's wire was busy. For a few uncomfortable seconds I waited and tried again. The wire continued busy and the line-up continued to stare. I am fairly adept at outstaring on occasions, but this didn't seem to be one of them. I was, however, damned if, under their searchlight scrutiny I'd wait with lowered eyelids until the phone was clear. Giving up any idea of announcing my arrival, I walked with womanly dignity over to the elevators and got into a car. The only other occupant, besides the operator was a gentleman wearing a convention plaque which announced his identity as being J. W. Truby. His manner indicated that the convivial aspects of the local convention must have been of twenty-four-hour continuity. The doors closed with a portentous clang and my heart sank in ratio to the elevator's rapid rise. I felt panicky and as if I'd have to turn to someone. Mr. Truby, perhaps. For an insane moment I struggled with the impulse to tell him what I was about to do. What quickly restrained me was the sobering thought that Mr. Truby might decide to come along with me and his presence would be difficult to explain to Dr. Kinsey. The elevator came to a stop and I hurried off.

The Pennsylvania-Statler is one of those hotels which employs gray-haired, highly respectable matrons who sit behind a desk on every floor, hand you your key, your mail and a motherly smile and, from their vantage positions, take discreet note of where you are going. These ladies, the Association of Innkeepers would lead us to believe, convey that "homey" touch, but to me, even under such innocent circumstances as when I am merely bound for my own room, they convey an undefinable sense of guilt. On this occasion the sense was more definable. I felt like a call-girl. Taking comfort in the thought that I didn't look at all like a call-girl . . . which as comfort was not too morale-building . . . I set my hat at a digni-fied angle, smiled cozily at the matron and started briskly for Dr. Kinsey's room, which proved to be in a direction completely opposite to where I was going. This involved repassing the desk and this time I avoided looking at the matron.

I found the room and I found Dr. Kinsey and him I found to be a scholarly gentleman of humor and charm. He put me completely at ease and the inter-view I had dreaded proved to be as simple as it was fascinating. I came away with a high opinion of Dr. Kinsey and I don't mind saying a pretty good one of myself.

It may be of interest to note in conclusion that, within the ensuing twenty-four hours, of those per-sons who had evinced such outraged scruples at the prospect of this interview, not one failed to call me up and say, "What did he ask you?" My answer to each and every one was the same: "If you think I'm going to tell you what he asked, you're as crazy as you would be if you think I will tell you what I answered!"